THE CARNIVAL STAGE

The Carnival Stage

Vicentine Comedy within

the Serio-Comic Mode

José I. Suárez

Rutherford ● Madison ● Teaneck
Fairleigh Dickinson University Press
London and Toronto: Associated University Presses

1000238480

Associated University Presses
440 Forsgate Drive
Cranbury, NJ 08512

Associated University Presses
25 Sicilian Avenue
London WC1A 2QH, England

Associated University Presses
P.O. Box 338, Port Credit
Mississauga, Ontario
Canada L5G 4L8

The paper used in this publication meets the requirements of the American National Standard for Permanence of Paper for Printed Library Materials Z39.48-1984.

Library of Congress Cataloging-in-Publication Data

Suárez, José I., 1951–
  The carinval stage : Vicentine comedy within the serio-comic
                                    mode
 / José I. Suárez.
      p. cm.
   Includes bibliographical references and index.
   ISBN 0-8386-3491-5 (alk. paper)
   1. Vicente, Gil, ca. 1470-ca. 1536—Criticism and interpretation.
 2. Carnival. 3. Satire—Classical influences. I. Title.
 PQ9252.S83 1993
 869.2'2—dc20   91-58948
                                                          CIP

Para minha filha, Amélia, que veio e nunca chegou

Contents

FOREWORD
John Esten Keller

José I. Suárez clearly lays down in his Introduction and succinctly sums up in his Concluding Remarks the ideas his book states. No preface therefore needs to repeat what he makes so evident. However, a preface can and should at least permit its writer to offer his criticism in the hope that it may generate interest and state in favorable terms what Suárez, out of modesty, could not. Also, it allows for a more general biographical, historical, and literary presentation of Gil Vicente than a specialist like Suárez generally offers.

While Gil Vicente has not been the subject of as many scholarly books in Portuguese studies as, say, has been the *Lusiads* of Camoens, or in Spanish studies as, say, Juan Ruiz, there has been enough written about Vicente to establish his importance as a significant writer. Even so, Suárez, conscious of previous studies and familiar with the considerable bibliography concerned with this dramatist, has produced an original work. He certainly approaches Vicente's drama in a refreshing, innovative, and valid way, and his interpretation goes beyond the usual critical view of scholars who have stressed the historical and traditional aspects of that drama, since he presents ideas that have not been articulated profoundly before.

As Suárez studies Menippean characteristics in Gil Vicente's plays, he fits specific plays into fourteen subdivisions that Mikhail Bakhtin deems essential to the Menippean satire, a fine example of the serio-comic genre. I find this satisfying, since it finally codifies the Vicentine opus.

Suárez's book, of course, takes into account the opinions and studies of other Vicentine scholars, as any thorough scholar would, but even so, when their works are invoked, it successfully enriches and more profoundly defines his views in comparison with or

9

contrast to theirs. His originality in part can be seen in his focusing upon less-studied aspects of Gil Vicente's dramaturgy, not that he neglects its broader limits. I have not found a more scholarly synthesis of Peninsular drama from its origins and the impact the popular element had on its formation.

José I. Suárez is one of the most respected of the new generation of scholars and one of the most scholarly. His book integrates traditional methods of investigation with more contemporary approaches, and it will continue to be regarded as an original facet in the overall complexity of Vicentine studies. The book is clear, concise, and direct in its presentation and is an example of sound and solid interpretation.

My own interest in Peninsular drama, both literary and popular, has inspired me to write this foreword and to state that I wish I could so carefully have researched and written a book as intuitive, original, and clearly presented as Suárez's.

Acknowledgments

Several people have contributed to this study in various ways. For this I am most grateful.

My wife, Kathy, gave me the support and love I needed to realize this project. I could not have done it without her.

Albert R. Lopes taught me Portuguese and made me a better teacher.

The late Jack E. Tomlins proposed the critical approach and provided advice.

The Fulbright Commission awarded the generous grant that enabled me to do much of the research in Lisbon, Portugal.

Clifford E. Landers's painstaking editing and invaluable suggestions improved the text.

My appreciation also goes to all other readers of the manuscript for their comments, observations, and corrections.

THE CARNIVAL STAGE

Introduction

Gil Vicente, it is theorized, was born either in Lisbon, Guimarães, or Barcelos between 1460 and 1470. Nothing is known about his early years. He arrived in Évora for the 1490 wedding of Crown Prince Afonso to Princess Isabel of Castile to ply the goldsmith's trade. Soon thereafter, under the tutelage of João II and Queen Leonor, his professional future was guaranteed. In 1509 Manuel I appointed him overseer of all gold and silver artifacts wrought for the Belém Monastery, the Templar Convent in Tomar, and All Saints Hospital in Lisbon. In 1513, he was promoted to Master of the Royal Mint, a position he occupied until 1517. In 1520, he was commissioned to organize the festivities in honor of the arrival in Lisbon of Queen Isabel, Manuel's third wife.

Although Vicente's educational background is undocumented, the philosophical and theological knowledge exhibited in his plays indicates some formal instruction. His deductive powers and oratory skills earned him respect, even among men he deemed ignorant and fanatical. The outcome of his 1531 sermon on tolerance, preached to monks at Santarém, attests to this. In it, he reprimanded clerics who maintained that faithlessness among "New Christians" (converted Jews) had angered God, prompting Him to devastate Lisbon by an earthquake. He prevented a pogrom by convincing both monks and laymen that the disaster was a natural phenomenon and not the sign of divine displeasure.

Details are few concerning Vicente's personal life. He wed twice: to Branca Bezerra around 1490 and, after her death, to Melícia Rodrigues in 1514. He had two sons by Branca (Gaspar and Belchior), and two daughters and a son by Melícia (Valéria, Paula, and Luís). The year of his death is unconfirmed, though scholars generally agree on 1537. They reason that because *Forest of Deceits* (Vicente's last play, in which he is believed to have acted the role of "Judge") was staged before the Court in Évora on December 1536 and because he is buried there, it is probable he died in that city soon thereafter.

In June 1502 Gil Vicente's dramatic career begins at court, the day after Prince João's birth, where he performed *The Herdsman's Monologue* (also known as *The Visitation*) for Queen Maria. This play and those which followed, *The Castilian Pastoral Play* (1502), *The Play of the Magi* (1503), and *The Play of St. Martin* (1504), are in Spanish and demonstrate the influence of the Salamancan School (Juan del Encina and Lucas Fernández): the main characters are shepherds who express themselves in dialectical *sayagués* (rustic Spanish).

After a five-year hiatus, Gil Vicente resumed his dramatic output with *The Play of India* (1509). Although not abandoning the Salamancan tradition, he began at this time to satirize Portuguese customs and introduced Portuguese into the composition. Later works showing the Salamancan influence include: *The Play of Faith* (bilingual, 1510), *The Play of the Four Seasons* (Spanish and *sayagués*, 1511), *The Play of the Sibyl Cassandra* (Spanish, 1513), *Who Has Bran?* (bilingual, 1515 or 1508), and *The Play of Mofina Mendes* (Portuguese, 1515 or 1534).

Remaining Vicentine plays will not be classified. For reasons to be made clear in this study, any classification is arbitrary and often controversial, contributing little to the understanding of the works. For this reason, they will be listed in chronological order (for disputed year of origin, the alternate year is also given), indicating the language(s) of composition: *The Play of the Fairies* (Portuguese with plurilingual games, 1511); *The Farce of the Old Man of the Orchard* (Portuguese, 1512); *The Exhortation of War* (Portuguese, 1514); *The Play of Fame* (plurilingual, 1515 or 1521); *The Ship of Hell* (Portuguese, 1516 or 1517); *The Soul's Journey* and *The Ship of Purgatory* (Portuguese, 1518); *The Ship of Heaven* (Spanish, 1519); *Courts of Jupiter* and *The Play of Rubena* (bilingual, 1521); *The Farce of the Gypsy Women* (Spanish, 1521 or 1525); *Dom Duardos* (Spanish, 1522 or 1525); *The Farce of Inês Pereira* (bilingual, 1523); *The Portuguese Pastoral Play* (Portuguese, 1523); *Amadis de Gaula* (Spanish, 1523 or 1533); *The Play of the Widower* (Spanish and *sayagués*, 1524 or 1514); *The Forge of Love* (bilingual, 1524); *The Play of the Doctors* (bilingual, 1524 or 1512); *The Farce of the Judge of Beira* and *The Festival Play* (bilingual, 1525); *The Farce of the Priest from Beira* (Portuguese, 1925); *The Temple of Apollo* (bilingual, 1526); *The Play of the Fair* (Portuguese, 1527 or 1528); *The Farce of the Carriers*, *The Pastoral Tragicomedy of the Estrela Mountain Range*, and *The History of God* (Portuguese, 1527); *The Ship of Love* and *The Play on the Coat of Arms of the City of Coimbra* (bilingual, 1527); *The Dialogue on the Resurrection* (Portuguese, 1527 or 1528); *The Triumph of Winter* (bilingual, 1929); *The Play of Lusitania* (bilingual,

1532); *The Pilgrimage of the Aggrieved* (Portuguese, 1533); *The Play of the Canaanite Woman* (Portuguese with plurilingual games, 1534); and *The Forest of Deceits* (bilingual, 1536).

These forty-four plays, in addition to exhibiting a degree of artistic sophistication unparalleled by Peninsular pieces of the era, reveal the social changes produced by the enormous needs of Portuguese overseas expansion. The centralization of power in Lisbon, the settling of newly acquired territories, the importation of black slaves, the constant need for manpower as crews for the outgoing ships—all this created political, military, social, and economic problems new to the experience of the tiny nation. In addition, Castile's imperialistic intentions to annex Portugal forced the Portuguese to look *além mar* to avoid being dominated. It was against this background that Gil Vicente originated an autochthonous Portuguese drama.   *aboriginal*

Let us now look briefly at how Gil Vicente satirized the social types of his day as they forfeited their virtues and adopted the corrupt and materialistic mentality exacted by a period of national insecurity and extraordinary personal demands.

Readily evident throughout the playlets is an endless gallery of characters representing the different classes and professions: kings, princes, priests, nobles of various degree, servants, farmers, shepherds, peddlers, muleteers, merchants, usurers, panderesses, warriors, artisans, sailors, cobblers, gardeners, doctors, lawyers, magistrates, blacksmiths, bakers, popes, among others. In fairness, though he made all these representatives of society the target of his mordant satire, he also praised them when warranted. These classes and professions will be divided into four categories for purposes of discussion: the nobility, the clergy, the professionals, and the common folk.

The Nobility

The nobility was particularly attacked; not the grand nobility on which the dramatist depended, but the lesser nobility composed of squires and poor nobles who sought out the court so that they might lead a futile and parasitic existence.

Besides the allusions to this petty nobility in several plays, Master Gil wrote one especially to criticize it. In the *Farsa dos Almocreves*, a noble refuses to pay his servants—a chaplain, a goldsmith, a page, and a muleteer—and finds a simple solution to all his financial difficulties: marrying a *dama de bom morgado*. These poor nobles formed part of a new social group: the victims of the rapidly eroding seignorial power base vis-à-vis an emerging capitalist middle class, the product of commercialization.

Vicente also criticized the poor squire, especially in the *Farsa do Juiz da Beira*, the *Farsa de Inês Pereira*, and *Quem Tem Farelos?* The latter was composed with this purpose partly in mind: Aires Rosado only leaves his house at night because he dresses poorly, while another squire in the play wears rented clothes. Despite surviving on rations of bread and radishes, Aires boasts of his wealth, particularly in the presence of women. The squire in the *Farsa de Inês Pereira*, who had gone *às partes de além* to become a knight and was killed by a Moorish shepherd as he fled the battlefield, like the poor nobles did not pay his servant but instead promised him a position at court. Another characteristic of these poor squires satirized by Master Gil was their obsession with music and poetry, which enabled them to seduce impressionable girls like Inês Pereira and Isabel.

The Clergy

The playwright openly attacked the clergy and, on occasion, certain abuses committed by the Church itself, as it too had been tainted by corruption. For this he was accused of being a follower of Erasmus, a charge that has given rise to much controversy among present-day scholars. Although his "pre-Reformational" attitude was energetic and adamant, he in no way suggested a break with the Church in Rome. He never condemned the Church as an institution, but limited his virulent attacks to what he considered its unfair policies and practices. Above all, he repeatedly criticized its representatives—the licentious priests and friars whose numbers were steadily rising as the need for laborers in agriculture and for colonization declined. It is precisely this that Friar Rodrigo expresses in the *Frágoa de Amor* when he decides to renounce his religious vows:

> Porque meu saber não erra:
> somos mais frades qu'a terra
> sem conto na Cristandade,
> sem servirmos nunca em guerra.[1]

The criticism goes on: in the *Romagem de Agravados*, side by side with the courtly Friar Paço, appears the ambitious Friar Narciso, who aspires to a bishopric; in the *Barca do Inferno* a Dominican friar, hand in hand with his concubine, enters dancing and singing; in the *Barca da Glória* a bishop, an archbishop, a cardinal, and a pope are damned until they are saved at the last moment by the figure of Christ; in the *Nau de Amores* there appears a Friar Martinho, who went mad because of love and at whom dogs barked day and night; in the *Auto dos Físicos* it is Friar Diogo who suffers from lovesickness; in the *Farsa de Inês Pereira* there are two friars who are less than moral exemplars; in the *Clérigo da Beira* the principal character converses with his son and shows more interest in chasing hares and young women than in saving souls. Medieval iconography provides the key to this hidden humorous symbolism.[2]

Other times, as in the *Auto das Fadas*, Master Gil presents us with clergymen delivering burlesque sermons or criticizes either their ignorance or their obsession with hollow erudition (*Auto da Mofina Mendes*). There is, among all this clerical debauchery, one friar who stands out as the exception: it is he who, in the *Comédia do Viúvo*, attempts to relieve the anguish of a man whose wife had recently died. Gil Vicente, beyond any doubt, would have wanted all friars to be thus.

The Professionals

Professional persons, such as judges and medical doctors, were not spared the lash of his constructive satire. He relentlessly attacked corruption within the judicial system by introducing magistrates, judges, and bailiffs who were ignorant, venal, and miserable swindlers. There are references to these dishonest officials in the *Farsa do Juiz da Beira*, the *Barca do Inferno*, and, particularly, in the *Frágoa de Amor* and the *Floresta de Enganos*. Observe just such a reference in the following excerpt from the *Frágoa de Amor*:

> Fazei-me estas mãos menores,
> que não possam apanhar,
> e que não possa escutar
> esses rogos de Senhores,
> que me fazem entortar.
>
> (4:118)

This is said by Justice, who approaches the forge "em figura de hũa velha corcovada, torta, muito mal feita, com sua vara quebrada," and whose hands, enormous in size, are accustomed to *apanhar*. She begs to be straightened out, a deed accomplished only after a pair of chickens, a pair of partridges, and two huge bags filled with money are extracted from her pockets. No doubt is left that these objects contributed much to her deformed hunchbacked, physical appearance.

In the *Floresta de Enganos*, a judge—Dr. Justiça Maior—disguised as a black slave with his face daubed with charcoal, is made to sift flour by a girl who had sought his counsel and whom he wanted to seduce. This character may be seen as an image, literally disguised, of a public figure whom Master Gil wished to deride. Luiz da Cunha Gonçalves raises this possibility:

> Nos reinados de D. Manuel I e D. João III foram Regedores das Justiças ou Justiças Maiores D. Fernando Coutinho da Silva, seu irmão Aires da Silva e o filho deste João da Silva. Seria algum destes o que figura na *Floresta de Enganos*? Talvez.[3]

The medical profession was thoroughly ridiculed in the *Auto dos Físicos*, composed with such a purpose in mind. A priest, madly in love with a girl by the name of Blanca Denisa, asks that his servant take her a letter. The servant returns informing him that she tore up the letter and refused to give an answer. The priest takes seriously ill. Immediately afterward, Brasia Dias appears and, after diagnosing the symptoms as those of a chill, prescribes that a hot tile be applied and that he:

> Tomai ora um suadouro
> de bosta de porco velho,
> e com unto de coelho
> esfregai o pousadeiro,

> (6:105)

These malodorous remedies having no healing effect on the patient, four well-known doctors of the time examine him in succession: Master Felipe, Master Fernando, Master Anrique, and Físico Torres (direct references to known contemporary figures). Each contradicts the others' diagnoses and, consequently, all differ on their prescriptions; yet all have one thing in common besides their profession: the reliance on a pet expression to communicate a point of view—"entendeis!" (Master Felipe), "ouvi-lo?" (Master Fernando), "habeis mirado?" (Master Anrique), and "si" or "segundo" (Físico Torres).

The doctors' incompetence and ignorance are manifested from the moment they open their mouths, since the audience knows the real cause of the priest's illness. Lest anyone forget, Gil Vicente puts these words in the mouth of the priest's servant:

Cant'eu não posso entender
estes físicos, senhor:
Vós sois doente de amor,
e eles querem-vos meter
per caminho de outra dor.

(6:119)

The Common Folk

The peasant who goes to the city or royal court only to be
fleeced (*Clérigo da Beira*) stands out among all the popular Vicentine
figures. It is he who bears the brunt of a society riddled with par-
asites and idlers. He is not, however, the ridiculous rustic who
arouses our sympathy in the pastoral plays, but "uma personagem
patética cuja voz acusadora tem acentos comoventes."[4]

In his simple language, he is able to disclose many truths that,
coming from anyone else, would not have been tolerated. In the
Romagem de Agravados, for example, João Mortinheira complains to
Friar Paço that God has ill will toward him. When the latter demands an explanation, he answers without fear:

Que chove quando não quero,
e faz um sol das estrelas,
quando chuva alguma espero.
  Ora alaga o semeado,
ora seca quanto i há
ora venta sem recado,
ora neva e mata o gado,
e ele tanto se lha dá.

(5:6)

The blasphemies continue, demonstrating his rebellion against a
life of suffering, a life that makes even Nature an adversary. In the
same play, there is a peasant who has lost all desire to sing because
he had had to make a payment on the land he was leasing from a
pair of Carthusian friars despite his difficult financial situation. In
the *Barca do Purgatório*, a peasant tells the angel that he deserves
Paradise because he had spent a life of deprivation:

Bofá, Senhor, mal pecado,
sempre é morto quem do arado
há de viver.
  Nos somos vida das gentes,
e morte de nossas vidas;

(2:93)

Besides the miserable peasant, there are other popular figures that do stand out throughout the plays: the usurer, the cobbler who fleeced the people, the blacksmith, the wench, the baker, the Jew who was both tax collector and moneylender, and the *ratinho* (country boy from Beira) who, aspiring to become a knight, would give up country life and go to Lisbon. To this list add the pander-esses (Genebra Pereira, Lianor Vaz, Branca Gil, Ana Dias, and Brisida Vaz), the gypsies, the midwives, the witches, the servants, the peddlers, and several others.

Yet though none of these groups was presented in a very favorable light, one must not think that there are only depraved stereotypes in Vicentine drama. In it one also catches sight of in-nocent children, of the chaste love of shepherds, of maternal good sense, and of compassion for the unfortunate, and, as has already been seen, especially for the peasants.

Attention must now be focused on major critical studies and principal editions of Gil Vicente's complete works in order to better understand the need for the present study.

Vicentine Scholarship and Editions

While in the process of preparing his *autos* for publication, Gil Vicente met his death (circa 1537). Twenty-five years later (1562), the playwright's son, Luís, published his father's works and, in com-pliance with the latter's wishes, dedicated them to the then-deceased John III. Thanks to this *editio princeps* entitled *Copilaçam de Todalas Obras de Gil Vicente*, the delightfully entertaining pieces of the "Father of Peninsular Drama" escaped oblivion.

Along with having polished the inherited plays and changed their chronology for publication, Luís Vicente was also responsible for their fourfold division into the *cosas de devaçam, comedias, tragico-medias,* and *farsas*. With this general yet primitive classification, he unknowingly became the first critic of his father's drama, attempting what no Vicentine scholar up to the present has accomplished: categorize the playlets by groups in accordance with the particular schematized distribution.

Because of the protection that Queen Catherine and Princess Mary gave this first edition, it was spared alteration by the censoring hand of the Inquisition that had found its way to Portugal by 1536. However, such was not the case with the second edition of the *Copilaçam*, edited by Afonso Lopes and made public in 1586. Many of the plays' verses in this edition were mutilated or deleted on grounds that their immoral and anticlerical content was heretical and counter to the Church's precepts and teachings.

For reasons that are unclear, Gil Vicente's compositions lay dormant for the next two hundred and fifty years. One may conjecture that the invasion of Portugal by Philip II of Spain in 1580 and the fears raised by both ecclesiastical and civil censorship did little to further the study or the publication of Vicentine drama. True, the second edition of the *Copilaçam* appeared during this period, but a comparison of its content with that of the original edition reveals the extent of the Holy Office's alterations. Portugal lived at a far remove from the modernizing cultural trends circulating throughout Europe (e.g., Decartes's *Discours de la méthode* [1637]) because, under the watchful eye of the Counter Reformation, Portuguese culture entered an era of creative sterility.

Amidst this sociocultural chaos arose a new artistic movement that would become known as the baroque. A medium for the ideology sanctioned by the Council of Trent and its most ardent advocate, the Jesuits, it was characterized by preference for exaggerated forms; preoccupation with artificiality in writing (paradoxes, puns, oxymorons, esoteric concepts, etc.), which lent a pompous tone that made it, at times, incomprehensible; and emphasis on moral and religious edification. Obviously, artistic concepts of this nature were unlikely to draw attention to the popular, satirical, often anticlerical dramas of Master Gil. On the other hand, his strictly religious plays were brought to the stage during this period because they accommodated the objectives of a Church threatened by the sweeping gains of the Reformation.

During mid-eighteenth century, a literary current that condemned the superficiality and obscurantism associated with the baroque began to take hold in the small kingdom. Neoclassicism sought to reinstate the classical Greco-Roman modes and reinstate sobriety and clarity in literary language. It shunned the native art and culture, preferring all that was French in origin. Such a transformation in the existing criteria relegated our poet-playwright's opus to gather dust until propitious circumstances could again bring it to national attention.

As a result of the absolutism of the reigning Braganzas, many liberals were forced into exile in the early 1800s. Among these were José V. Barreto Feio and José Gomes Monteiro, two young men who, at the library of the University of Göttingen, came upon a copy of the first edition of the *Copilaçam* and decided, "movidos de amor que sempre tiveram pelas nossas cousas," to disseminate it through a reedition.[5] It must be noted, however, that literarily this period was most propitious for a revival of Gil Vicente's work. The various democratic and libertarian movements of early nineteenth-century Europe associated themselves with romanticism, a belletristic current that traced its roots to the German *Sturm und Drang* movement.

Among its many revolutionary and unconventional characteristics was the strong propensity of romanticism to seek refuge in the national past of the respective countries. The Middle Ages, with its poetry and chivalric demeanor, its Christian mystique and popular folklore, provided the romantic writer a wealth of thematic resources. Consequently, the new edition of Gil Vicente's complete works that came off the press in 1834 in Hamburg was not only the result of a fortuitous discovery by two Portuguese exiles, but also of the desire by men of letters to escape a reality of uncertainty and political unrest.

The 1834 edition restored Vicentine drama to the Portuguese stage and sparked an interest that engendered studies of the playwright's life and work. Early in this century, the first Portuguese edition (Coimbra) finally appeared after a gap of over three hundred years: Mendes dos Remédios wrote a preface and glossary for his edition entitled *Obras de Gil Vicente*, published in three separate volumes (1907, 1912, and 1914). The playlets are grouped according to the language in which they were written: first volume, Portuguese works; second volume, bilingual works; third volume, Spanish works. This runs counter to chronological order, as most of Gil Vicente's earliest production was written entirely in Spanish.

In order to aid scholarly research, the Biblioteca Nacional published in 1928 a facsimile of its copy of the original *Copilaçam*. This facsimile must not have been closely proofread inasmuch as it contains errors that lead to utter perplexity. Stephen Reckert cautions that the photocopy taken from retouched negatives does not give an accurate reproduction of the extant copy; although various errors were corrected, others were accidentally introduced.[6] Take for instance the scene in the *Auto dos Reis Magos* in which the shepherd Gregorio warns his companion Valerio to listen closely to what the nobleman, whom Valerio has just insulted, has to say. Valerio readily admits his impudence and apologizes to the nobleman. In the facsimile edition, the roles become illogically reversed, for here it is Valerio who warns Gregorio, with the latter seeking the nobleman's pardon; however, Valerio remains the shepherd who was originally disrespectful.

This discrepancy seems not to exist in the copy of the *editio princeps* discovered in Göttingen. The 1834 edition, derived from it, correctly matches all speakers with their corresponding lines. In spite of these recurring *lapsus calami*, the facsimile edition even today serves as the basis for all Vicentine studies.

The decades of the fifties and sixties proved fruitful for new editions of Gil Vicente's complete works. Costa Pimpão makes the only attempt, to date, to offer a critical edition of the Vicentine opus in *Obras Completas de Gil Vicente* (Barcelos, 1956); Marques Braga created the most popular compilation, based on his excellent introduction, notes, and glossary, for which reason it is the edition employed in this study; from Porto, a one-volume collection entered the market in 1965 printed on *papel bíblia* and with no reference to its editor or arbitrary textual order; Reis Brasil's edition of 1966 attempts to aid the general reader by a supplementary prose rendering of every playlet, thus revealing their fine detail and *amplidão de sentido*; in 1983, Maria Leonor Carvalhão Buescu publishes an edition in modern print of the original *Copilaçam*.

Though many studies were published during the nineteenth century, the most notable is Teófilo Braga's "Gil Vicente e as Origens do Teatro Nacional," which formed a part of his *História da Literatura Portugueza* (Porto, 1898). In the words of J. H. Parker, it is "an old-fashioned but basically sound general study of the beginning of the Portuguese theater."[7] The literary historian briefly examines existing documented data concerning the poet's life and speculates on possible literary antecedents to some of the Vicentine pieces and their influence on subsequent works. While concluding that Gil Vicente was an extraordinary exponent of Portuguese tradition and sentiment, he invites controversy by asserting that the poet Gil Vicente and a goldsmith by that name who appears in court documents of the period were not the same individual. This weakly sustained argument gave rise to Anselmo Braamcamp Freire's monumental investigation *Vida e Obras de Gil Vicente "Trovador, Mestre da Balança"* (Lisbon, 1919).

This study, besides making a good case for the assumption that the goldsmith and the poet were one, offers a detailed three-part biography of Master Gil: prior to his first presentation (1460?-1502), during the reign of Manuel I (1502-21), and during the reign of John III (1521-57). The scholar sets forth the relationship between these distinct periods and the dramatist's work, accompanied by a detailed presentation of the effect of Inquisitional censorship on the two sixteenth-century compilations and on the extant loose editions. It should be noted, however, that an entire chapter is devoted to underscoring the fact that not all contextual differences among the existing versions of a given play are attributable to the Holy Office; some stem from the divergence among the originals consulted in the making of the reproductions. The study ends with an invaluable section containing all of the documents discovered to that time in which Gil Vicente's name appears, which are essential in the determination of his identity.

While Braamcamp Freire was putting the final touches on his work, another Vicentine scholar was preparing a biographical study of her own. Carolina Michaëlis de Vasconcelos shed new light on certain aspects of Master Gil's life and literary influence by an empirical analysis of all surviving facts. *Notas Vicentinas*, the title of this *magnum opus* published in Lisbon in 1921, is composed of five "notes" that neither generalize the topics nor overlap with Braamcamp Freire's observations. Consequently, between the two studies, much biographical, historical, chronological, and bibliographical data have been gathered regarding the conundrum that Gil Vicente and his drama pose for modern scholars.

Two other towering figures have written fact-oriented Vicentine studies. Óscar de Pratt, in *Gil Vicente: Notas e Comentários* (Lisbon, 1931), employed the same "note" format as Carolina Michaëlis de Vasconcelos; although less extensively researched, it offers noteworthy insights into the chronology, classification, and purpose of several playlets along with biographical commentaries on the dramatist. Paul Teyssier is author of *La langue de Gil Vicente* (Paris, 1959), a stylistic and linguistic investigation indispensable to those seeking a sound understanding of Master Gil's literary language, whether Portuguese or Spanish.

All these studies employ one of two approaches: biographical /bibliographical (basing observations and conclusions on surviving historical information concerning the author and his work) and/or philological (to study his poetic language and structure in accordance with recorded sixteenth-century accepted usage). Other, more theoretical, studies analyze the man and his work in relationship to the historical setting, attempting to explain the Vicentine phenomenon as the product of a particular era. Perhaps the most reputable study of this type is António J. Saraiva's doctoral dissertation, *Gil Vicente e o Fim do Teatro Medieval*, published in Lisbon in 1942. It assigns new categories (*gêneros*) to the plays because the original categorization by Luís Vicente was not to Saraiva's satisfaction. This purely external categorization approach does not escape the pitfalls and shortcomings encountered when thematic and internal characteristics are ignored. Categorizing of this sort unfortunately overlooks any superposition of categories as occurs in the *Auto da Fé*, which on the one hand has all the trademarks of a morality play while, on the other, resembling Encina's eclogues.[8]

By pointing out textual similarities between given Vicentine pieces and earlier Castilian and, particularly, French theatrical compositions, Saraiva demolishes the supposition that Gil Vicente's drama sprang *ex nihilo.* To him, Gil Vicente was not an originator but a renovating continuator made possible by the replacement, during the waning of the Middle Ages, of a disintegrating symbolic unity by the allegoric. Hence, he argues, the founder of Portuguese theater must be appreciated and understood within a late medieval framework.

Were one to accept the above conclusion unconditionally, how to explain the delight that a read or staged comedy of Master Gil imparts to a modern audience? Is it not the universal rather than the medieval element that accounts for this? Eighteen years later, in his *Para a História da Cultura em Portugal* (Lisbon, 1960), Saraiva recants his original thesis by admitting that "na arte medieval existiram formas que nem por terem sido desprezadas após o Renascimento deixam de ser formas válidas que a Idade Média de modo algum sepultou" (2:314-15).

Just as in the earlier study, the Portuguese critic utilizes a comparative method to illustrate his affirmation: the striking correlation between Master Gil's *Farsa do Juiz da Beira* and Bertolt Brecht's *The Caucasian Chalk Circle*. One, a medieval playlet by a dramatist from the westernmost tip of Europe; the other, a contemporary piece by one of Central Europe's most acclaimed playwrights. But, aside from the seemingly coincidental similarities that abound in these specific works, both authors share the same genre, derive their contents from the popular sector, and repeatedly criticize the establishment via satire. It was precisely this last work by Saraiva, along with Mikhail Bakhtin's theories on the genre-formative effect of carnival (the serio-comic genres), that prompted the present study. Another study worthy of mention is René P. Garay's recently published *Gil Vicente and the Development of the "Comedia"*. This extraordinary work traces the development of the *comedia* from antiquity to the Vicentine era and provides a systematic analysis and interpretation of *Comédia de Rubena* and *Comédia do Viúvo*. Let us turn to Bakhtin's theories on the impact of popular festivities on literature to obtain an understanding of their formulation.

Bakhtin's Viability

Mikhail Bakhtin's literary theories have been more widely disseminated and acclaimed in the West than those of his contemporaries. His popularity is largely attributable to his convincing modern studies on Fedor Dostoevsky and François Rabelais.

Published in 1929 under the title *Problems of Dostoevsky's Creative Art*, his monograph on the Russian novelist reveals that his works, unlike Tolstoy's, are "polyphonic" because we hear in them many voices but are unable to pinpoint the voice of Dostoevsky. This technical achievement makes Dostoevsky the creator of a totally new novelistic genre, one unknown to writers of the same period. It may be validly argued that Cervantes preceded Dostoevsky in the creation of a truly polyphonic novel; after all, *Don Quixote's* many characters offer a plurality of voices none of which can be directly attributed to the author. Bakhtin does concede that Dostoevsky is not unique in the history of the novel and that his polyphonic novel is not exempt from forebears. But he is also of the opinion that, whereas Cervantes, together with Shakespeare, Rabelais, Grimmelshausen, et al., belongs to that line of development in European literature in which the seeds of polyphony culminated, it is Dostoevsky who occupies the apex. By listing only the shortcomings of drama (Shakespearean) with relation to a completely formed and deliberate polyphony, the Russian theorist avoids an explanation as to why Cervantes's multivoiced novel does not qualify as a full-fledged polyphonic *oeuvre*.[9]

One may readily see in his approach the critic's affiliation with the formalist school: his primary concern is with the novels themselves, with the fundamental aspects of their aesthetic forms, not with the author's biography or psychology. But, clearly under the influence of Schlovsky's critical analysis of *War and Peace*, Bakhtin's book on Dostoevsky likewise reflects the second phase of the formalist school's development—the incorporation of Marxist socioideological considerations—inasmuch as the Russian critic, upon deducing that Dostoevsky's polyphonic novels have as a foundation an atypical nineteenth-century plot composition and are linked to other traditions of genre in the development of European prose, felt compelled to throw light upon this question from the standpoint of the genre's history. That is, he shifts his consideration to the realm of historical poetics (not to be confused with traditional "historicism"), where he sets out to trace the sources of Dostoevsky's tradition of genre back to antiquity. What had to that point been largely a synchronic, formalist analysis (Dostoevsky's work) suddenly becomes a diachronic, Marxist analysis (Dostoevsky's genre tradition: the carnivalized serio-comic genres). In her foreword to Bakhtin's *Rabelais and His World*, Krystyna Pomorska attributes this digression by the scholar to his attraction to the structural theories of Tynianov and Jakobson, which predicated that any part must be analyzed in relationship to its whole, e.g., a work within the tradition of genre to which it belongs.[10] Bakhtin explains his digression as follows:

> Having linked Dostoevsky with a specific tradition, it goes without saying that we have not in the slightest degree limited the profound originality and individual uniqueness of his work. Dostoevsky is the creator of *authentic polyphony*, which, of course, did not and could not have existed in the Socratic dialogue, the ancient Menippean satire, the medieval mystery play, in Shakespeare and Cervantes, Voltaire and Diderot, Balzac and Hugo. But polyphony was prepared for in a *fundamental* way by this line of development in European literature. (*Dostoevsky*, 178)

All in all, by relying primarily on theory (both diachronical and synchronical), the study—republished in 1963 under the altered title of *Problems of Dostoevsky's Poetics*—offers a valid interpretation of Dostoevsky's innovative opus.

Twelve years after the first edition of his monograph on Dostoevsky, Bakhtin wrote a monograph entitled *Rabelais and His World*. Lamentably, it did not reach the Russian reading public until 1965. The work demonstrates Bakhtin's increased inclination to view a literary text from a sociological perspective while in no way renouncing formalist norms. His overall intent is still purely theoretical: to show the oneness and meaning of folk humor, its general ideological, philosophical, and aesthetic essence as contained in Rabelais's work, and, conversely, to provide a clearer picture of the work and the man. Both have been persistently misunderstood by critics who have scrutinized them through modern lenses, ignoring Rabelais's ties to folk culture.

In Bakhtin's convincing argument, both Rabelais and Dostoevsky were exponents and renovators of a genre tradition with sources that can be traced back to the early festivals and rites associated with carnival. During this period, all social barriers were lifted in order to create the illusion of a classless society. Individuals from all walks of life, ignoring the official seriousness of the noncarnival world, came together in a carefree atmosphere, one made possible at a communicative level by the borrowed speech and gestures of the marketplace. There people customarily dealt with each other on a familiar plane.

The marketplace familiarities incorporated into carnival were not in themselves hilarious, but, counterposed to the formality and seriousness of the official world, they took on a comic nature and became ambivalent. Also, by no means restricted to verbal exchange, the ambivalent serio-comical language of carnival encompassed the marketplace's complex amalgam of symbols, gestures, and attitudes. Bakhtin maintains this language cannot be fully translated into verbal language, but can be transposed into literary language.

It was precisely the transposition of this language into the literary sphere that gave rise in antiquity to the serio-comic genres. Just as carnival fulfilled the social need to break temporarily with the monolithic seriousness of the status quo, the newly created genres (e.g., the Old Attic Comedy and the Menippean satire), manifesting the inherent humor of the folk, provided a badly needed alternative to the serious genres: the tragedy and the epic.

In his monograph on Dostoevsky Bakhtin restricted his comments on the impact of carnivalized literature on Russian prose to one chapter; in *Rabelais and His World* he devotes the entire volume to exemplifying the broad use of carnival imagery and language in the novelist's work. Although he does not directly state it, Bakhtin implies repeatedly that the characteristics of the Menippean or, for that matter, of any connected genre, are contained in Rabelais's production for it shares the common denominator of folk humor. He places Rabelais among the foremost transposers of the popular tradition onto the written page.

The present study is an attempt to trace the roots of Gil Vicente's dramatic or theatrical production to their proper sources. Initially, a broad look is given to the extant data concerning the origins of drama in the Iberian Peninsula, in both the secular and liturgical spheres. Absent any convincing evidence of true drama prior to the Portuguese dramatist's time, and with the opinion that early theatrical attempts were of a popular nature, attention shifts to Bakhtin's theories of the impact of carnival (here understood as any popular seasonal festivity) on the serio-comic genres, e.g., the Old Attic Comedy and the Menippean satire.

Because of the striking similarities between the antique Menippean satire (a highly carnivalized genre) and the Vicentine pieces, a detailed exemplification of the characteristics of the former as contained in the latter is offered. This leads to the conclusion that, although Master Gil was probably unaware of the Greek satires, or, for that matter, of its relative, the Aristophanic comedy, his opus shares one essential quality with these ancient genres: its origins are carnivalesque and it may therefore be included within the realm of the serio-comical. Naturally, the author investigated the possibility of motifs found in Stith Thompson's *Motif-Index of Folk Literature*, but without result. John E. Keller, whose *Motif-Index of Medieval Spanish Exempla* contains more than a thousand motifs, does not find parallels with motifs in the works of Gil Vicente. His is the only motif-index of Peninsular material. Alfred B. Lord's *The Singer of Tales*, which deals with folk epic material, did not yield motifs found in Vicente's plays. The need for a motif-index of Vicente and, indeed, for the entire corpus of Spanish drama, is great.

1

The Origins of Peninsular Drama

Although it is generally agreed that with the *Monólogo do Vaqueiro* Gil Vicente founded the Portuguese theater in 1502—if one can rely on the information furnished in the rubric of the play—it is naive to suppose that the poet-playwright sprang *ex nihilo*. That he was indeed influenced by the Salamancan School is no longer doubted, but it must be noted that these dramatists were his contemporaries and thus did not represent a long-standing tradition of written plays. However, a perusal of the extant works attributed to the Spaniards and the Portuguese reveals that such an inchoate esthetics of the drama was, no doubt, the culmination of a tendency preexisting in the Peninsula for several generations.

The lack of written material with which to identify this tendency does not constitute an exception to universal literary history. Early belletristic manifestations are commonly oral, and only after undergoing a required maturation process do they arrive on the written stage. Homer was both the apogee and the scribe of an oral tradition that anteceded the *Iliad* and the *Odyssey* by many decades. The techniques employed in these two classic epics had, therefore, been progressively perfected by the wandering poets who earned their keep recounting the deeds and exploits of legendary heroes. Memorization was simplified by the use of verse, and the narration underwent content variations to comply with the audience's demands.

Like Homer, the early Iberian dramatists must have embodied and perfected an oral tradition active for several centuries and thus formed an integral part of the folk entertainment. Unlike their Greek predecessor, however, these dramatists were revitalizing an ancient art form, the epitome of which are the accomplished comedies of Aristophanes, Menander, Plautus, and Terence.[1]

It is common knowledge that in the waning days of Rome, as staging techniques gradually improved, the quality of the productions concurrently deteriorated to placate the lower classes' insatiable desire for unrefined amusement. Such degeneration provoked a strong reaction from the early Christian Church that led to the closing of all theaters in the empire. The underlying motive, however, was the threat a pagan theater posed to the ill-defined cultural mentality of early Christians.[2] They must be thoroughly indoctrinated, and anything that maintained the pagan doctrines impaired the assimilation of the new Christian ideology.

The closing of theaters did not imply complete extinction of the *mimi*, as the Roman actors were designated, who had outlived the tragedy and the comedy, and were destined to outlive the stage. After the barbarian invasions and the fall of Rome, the *mimi* perforce became wandering entertainers performing buffooneries, pantomimes, satirical parodies, and dances wherever an audience would gather.[3] In these *homines vagantes* are found the ancestors of the medieval *joculatores* and *remedadores*. Later we shall return to this subject.

Whether theater in the Iberian Peninsula emerged fourteen centuries later from the legacy of these roving players or, as is believed to have occurred in the rest of Europe, from religious presentations performed within the confines of medieval churches, is indeed difficult to ascertain; no conclusive documented proof has been unearthed. In any case it may be stated that, before the Spanish primitives and Gil Vicente, there is no evidence of a clearly defined dramatic tradition in Peninsular theater.

This chapter will investigate both the liturgical and the profane representations of the Iberian Middle Ages. It is the author's intention to present what has been gathered by various scholars in the hope that Bakhtin's literary theories of genre based on European oral carnival folklore may be more feasibly applied. The object of this presentation, therefore, is to illustrate how drama emerged and survived outside the theater, not to demonstrate a lack of connection between Gil Vicente and early drama.

The Liturgical Drama

Western drama finds its most important source in the religious rites of its early civilizations. In ancient Greece, classical theater is thought to have arisen from the performances at the festivals of the Dionysian cult. In 535 B.C., Thespis is said to have presented his plays at the Great Dionysian in Athens, and in so doing, marked the official beginning of dramatic contests.[4] Likewise, modern drama formally originated with liturgical rites performed in the churches and monasteries of medieval Europe.

During the early part of the tenth century, the European Church, to embellish its liturgy, introduced tropes consisting of short dialogues in Latin, sung antiphonally between priest and choir.[5] These compositions, however, the origins of which date from fifth-century Byzantine liturgy, were not dramatic *in limine* since they were merely sung at Mass and lacked representational qualities. Not until the participants impersonated the biblical figures symbolized in the Easter trope (the first tropes known deal with the Resurrection) could these even vaguely be labeled "dramatic." It is likely that this impersonation did not arise until the trope was shifted from a position before the introit of the Mass to one following the conclusion of Matins.[6] With this shift, the trope came between the final Response and the concluding *Te Deum*. No climax followed it, the jubilation of the final hymn could be postponed, and the trope had sufficient time and place to develop.[7]

Since, chronologically speaking, the Christmas trope appears later (first texts date from the second half of the eleventh century; in the Iberian Peninsula these did not surface until the twelfth century at Huesca), it may be conjectured that it developed by analogy with the Resurrection trope.[8]

The adaptation did not require radical structural or linguistic alternation, as the juxtaposition of the following corresponding lines denotes:

> Quem queritis in sepulchro, o Christicolae?
> [Whom do you seek in the tomb, oh Christians?]
> Quem queritis in praesepe, pastores, dicite?
> [Whom do you seek in the manger, shepherds?]
>
> Jesum Nazarenum crucifixum.
> [Jesus of Nazareth, the crucified.]
> Salvatorem Christum Dominum.
> [Christ, our Lord and Savior.]
>
> Non est hic.
> [He is not here]
> Adest hic.
> [He is here][9]

Very few of the *Officia pastorum*, as the Christmas tropes are generally known, evolved into plays at Matins. It was at Lauds that the antiphon *Quem vidistis, pastores, dicite* or *Pastores, dicite, quidnam vidistis* took on quasi-dramatic effects. The contemporary medieval scholar William Tydeman substantiates this statement with the ensuing description:

> Five or seven youths played the shepherds, two priests the midwives, a choirboy the angel, while others formed the heavenly host. At the Mass which followed, the shepherds took a leading part in the singing of the responses and at the Office of Lauds they responded in character once more to the choir's question, "*Quem vidistis, pastores, dicite?*" with the words "*Natum vidimus et choros angelorum*". Indeed it was at Lauds that the *pastores* played their fullest role in the liturgical celebrations of Christmas.[10]

The brief but enlightening work of Richard B. Donovan has expanded the small number of studies on this primitive dramatic form in the medieval Iberian liturgy. By Iberian, one must understand the area west of Catalonia. From about the year 800, the religious, cultural, and political life of Catalonia was heavily influenced by France, which following the campaigns of Charlemagne, established its supremacy in the region.

The French-Roman rite thus took root in Catalonia approximately 250 years before its implantation in the remainder of the Iberian Peninsula, which was still under Arabic domination during this era. Not until 1075 did the French-Roman rite find its way to Castile, replacing a Mozarabic rite that, as far as extant records show, had no dramatic aspects in its liturgy.

That the *Auto de los reyes magos* came to light relatively soon afterward does not constitute proof that, with the new liturgy, drama quickly evolved and blossomed throughout the Peninsula. The source of the *Auto* may be, as Winifred Studervant keenly observed in her study, not the liturgical presentations but the French narrative poems and plays of the Infancy.[11]   Rafael Lapesa, analyzing the *Auto*'s rhyme scheme, lent credence to Studervant's allegation when he observed that the irregularities in the fragment must be attributed to a non-native speaker of Castilian. She traced the linguistic peculiarities to the area of France known as Gascony.[12]

Donovan concludes that this vernacular influence, along with the reforming spirit of the Cluniac monks who were responsible for the introduction of the new rite in the Peninsula, accounts for the lack of liturgical drama west of Catalonia. Nonetheless, this does not explain the total dramatic lacuna between the *Auto* and the rudimentary Nativity play of Gómez Manrique in the latter half of the fifteenth century.

The reason for this apparent lack of an autochthonous drama might have been the intentional disregard of the Church for any presentation that did not lend itself to reproduction in its highly ritualistic Latin liturgy.   Consequently, any play composed in the native tongue would not have been transcribed by the clerics. If we recall that much of the information on medieval art was discovered in churches and monasteries, this oversight would explain the absence of vernacular plays for that period. The fact that a fragment of the text of the *Auto* was found in the Cathedral of Toledo does not demonstrate that it was ever staged there or elsewhere, for nothing in the play itself suggests it was composed for this purpose.[13]

It is not, therefore, surprising that out of the eighty-five extant liturgical manuscripts pertaining to the Cathedral of Toledo, not one contains a single liturgical piece with which to associate the *Auto*. This fact does not prove their nonexistence, but if there were any, they were quite infrequent. In his *Las siete partidas*, Alphonse the Wise mentions *autos* that are befitting for staging by clerics during Christian holidays (the corresponding fragment of this thirteenth-century work will be quoted below). His statement, however, does not verify the existence of liturgical drama as such in the area; without the *autos* themselves, and these may be lost or never recorded, their contents cannot be determined.   Of importance is also González López's conclusion based on his legal background:

> The Wise King... took on the more ambitious project of creating a new body of laws that would take in those new and advanced doctrines being circulated throughout Europe by the Roman-law experts of the Bologne School: a body of laws that would serve not only as the standard for the kingdom's legislation, but also as a guiding light for the new generations of jurists to whom fell the arduous task of organizing and structuring the State with a national sense.[14]

If this was true, then Alphonse the Wise was referring to a European reality and not necessarily to Spain's.

A fourteenth-century breviary from Toledo, currently at Monserrat, contains directions for the dramatization of Christmas Lauds that, although not in the vernacular (Castilian may have been used in the actual presentation), exemplify the existence of the dramatized antiphon in the Peninsula:

> If by chance the Shepherds' Performance was staged, at the moment the angel announced to the shepherds that Christ was born, the psalm was sung, *laudate dominum de celis usque ad laudate dominum in sanctis eius*; meanwhile, boys dressed as shepherds were ready at the altar. Then, the two singers who led the choir would begin the antiphon *pastores dicite*. The boys would answer *Infantem vidimus*, and then *laudate dominum in*

sanctis eius was sung. Thus the antiphon was repeated verse by verse so that the above was sung continuously to the end of the psalm.[15]

In the above transcription, characterization reached an unprecedented stage in the Iberian evolution of drama: no longer would the shepherd's participation in the presentation be imagined. Henceforth, he would appear as a fully visual dramatic entity, i.e., an individual donning shepherd's garb. At this very stage, the prototype was established that would begin its search for an author to give it the traits required for its development as a full-fledged character. However, this did not occur immediately; he, the shepherd, had to remain a sterile participant in an even more sterile production until the schism came about that would enable him to surpass the confines of the Church. In so doing, this potentially comic figure would rid itself of the developmental restraints of ecclesiastical dogma. The breakthrough most likely occurred when the religious productions, having incorporated certain profane characteristics—a limited use of the vernacular, dancing, burlesque sermons, etc.—became too irreverent for a medieval Church with a low degree of tolerance. Measures then must be taken to curtail frivolity and restore propriety to the ceremony, but by then the congregation had acquired a taste for the amusement that such elements provided. The following excerpt from *Las siete partidas* gives an idea of the notoriety of these presentations in the thirteenth century, inasmuch as the king was compelled to ban them legally:

> nor should they be involved with farcical plays so that people may attend them and hear them. If other men perform these things, ecclesiatics should not be present, because many evil speeches are uttered and indecencies committed there; nor should any such things take place in churches, for we have previously declared that those who act in this manner should dishonorably be ejected from them, since the church of God is made to pray in, and not for the purpose of uttering farcical speeches.... There are certain representations, however, which ecclesiastics have a right to perform, for instance that of the birth of Our Lord Jesus Christ, in which is shown how the angel appeared to the shepherds and told them that Jesus Christ was born; and also that of his appearance, and how the three kings of the Magi came to adore him; and the one relating to his resurrection, which shows that he was crucified, and on the third day arose. Representations of this kind, which induce men to do good and have devotion for the faith, ecclesiastics can perform; and they are also beneficial, for they cause men to remember that the other events actually happened. These things should be done in an orderly way, and with great devotion, and should take place in large cities where there are archbishops or bishops, and either by their command, or by

those of others who occupy their places; and they should not take place in villages, or in vile places, or for the sake of earning money by means of them.[16]

Therefore, it may be inferred from this edict that not only were the presentations in Castilian, as the performances of such *juegos* seem to indicate, but also that they tended to take place in areas removed from the large urban centers, in villages where the Church's jurisdiction was less effective. (The term *juego* as used here must be interpreted to mean "jocose diversion" and is not to be confused with the French *jeu* which, during the thirteenth century, signified "drama" as may be verified in the *Jeu d'Adam*.) Did these marginal pieces constitute the formation of a secular religious drama maintained in a purely oral fashion? Were they entirely eradicated? Not at all. A canon from the Council of Arcanda (1473) indicates that the *juegos de escarnio* persisted in houses of worship and appear to have tainted the metropolitan clergy:

> Because of a certain custom tolerated in metropolitan churches and cathedrals in our province, scenic plays [i.e., *juegos escénicos*], masks, monsters, spectacles, and other diverse fictional accounts, all of equal impropriety, are represented in church during the celebrations of Saint Stephen, Saint John and All Saints Day, as well as during certain [other] holidays; also during the solemnity of a new mass (while the divine service is being held). And because in these events there is turmoil, and crude songs and burlesque sermons are heard to the point of disturbing the divine service and turning people irreligious, all of us present, with Council approval, hereby unanimously forbid this corrupt practice and the inclusion of said masks, plays, monsters, spectacles, fictional accounts, and turmoil, as well as the crude songs and illicit sermons...; likewise, we decree that those clerics who combine said forms of entertainment with divine service, or who indirectly agree to them..., shall be punished.... Let it not be understood by this that we also forbid those religious and devout presentations that inspire devotion in people either on set days or any other.[17]

One thing must be made clear: once successful entertainment forms became fixed (with primitive dramatic traits), clergymen, no matter how unsympathetic to profane amusement, must have seen some gain in introducing these forms into their services and endorsing their development.

The description of what may have been one of the ceremonies mentioned above, though much abated, is contained in the *Memorias i disertaciones que podrán servir al que escriba la historia de la iglesia de Toledo desde el año MLXXXV en que conquistó dicha ciudad el rei*

Don Alonso VI de Castilla of Felipe Fernández Vallejo. Vallejo believed that the ceremony that he copied from a manuscript of Juan Chaves de Arcayos, prebendary at the Cathedral of Toledo between 1589 and 1643, could very well represent an ancient dramatic tradition. In his opinion, the original *Officium pastorum* was brought into Spain from eleventh-century Benedictine monasteries and the Castilian *coplas* at the end were added at some time in the thirteenth century.[18] The description reads:

> At the onset of Mass, Priests step out of the Sacrarium dressed as Shepherds and go to the High Altar through the Wicket, and, up on its flat part, they dance while Mass is said; at the conclusion of Mass, said Disguised Prebendaries put on Capes to perform Lauds Service, which begins immediately in the Choir, and for which the Bell Ringer rings the bells with the Choir's cord, in accordance with custom, following a signal, once the *Te Deum laudamus* Hymn is sung; and, the Prester having sung *Deus in adjutorium* from his chair, the first antiphon is begun, which is: *Quem vidistis Pastores*; it is sung in its entirety, and then the Priests dressed as Shepherds and directed by their Cloister Master sing in the Main Choir, under the silver Lamp and during the Plainsong, the line *Infantem vidimus Pannis involutum, et Choros Angelorum laudantes salvatorem*, and repeat the entire antiphon: *Quem vidistis?* and the the Shepherds, between the two Choirs and beneath the middle Lamp, answer with the line *Infantem vidimus, ut supra*, and afterwards repeat the entire antiphon for the third time *Quem vidistis?* and the Shepherds, from the Door of the Archbishop's Choir, answer with the line *Infantem*, and then the Priests leave with their gilded Capes and their Sceptres, and they come up to the sides of the Eagle of the Archbishop's Choir and there the Singers, in Plainsong, ask them the following questions, and the Priests hold hands with two of those little Shepherds and ask them, along with the Singers, the following:

Plainsingers.	Welcome Shepherds,
	Welcome indeed.
	Where were you, Shepherds?
	Tell us what you saw?
Singers.	Welcome indeed.[19]

That dancing shepherds were allowed in the Toledan liturgy as late as the sixteenth century seems at odds with the strict Cluniac restrictions and the subsequent religious and monarchical reforming tendencies. Vallejo himself noted that in the eighteenth century this custom had been abolished owing to "certain abuses" (which he failed to specify).[20] It is likely that one of two possible events might have taken place: either the shepherds' dancing was not considered irreverent and was thus permitted, or because of pressures exerted by the congregation the practice was reinstated in the ceremony after an absence. Both suppositions are plausible, though it is impossible to determine which of the two, if either, actually occurred. Donovan adds substance to this argument when, observing that there is no record of a dancing shepherd in any non-Peninsular liturgy, he concludes that "religious dancing was always especially popular in Spain, and the provision for it in the document [Vallejo's] before us probably represents a traditional Spanish custom" and adds that "some have held that this usage dates back to the time of the Mozarabic rite."[21] It is of interest that both Chrysostom and Augustine frowned upon the Jewish sabbath dance: "melius enim utique tota die foderent, quam tota die saltarent."[22]

No mention of a liturgical drama in Portugal has been made as yet. If this type of drama was rare in Castile, it was even more so in Gil Vicente's native land. Not until relatively recently was one brief liturgical Christmas play discovered in a fourteenth-century breviary from the monastery of the Holy Cross of Coimbra. This little shepherd presentation at Lauds, comparable to the one found in the fourteenth-century Toledan breviary, is here intercalated in the description made by its discoverer, Solange Corbin. She writes:

> Psalter num. 1151 of the Municipal Library of Oporto, however, offers us a short Pastoral that takes place at Lauds on Christmas night. The classical antiphon is directed at the Shepherds' song *Pastores, dicite quidnam vidistis et anunciate Christi navitatem.* Here the rubric indicates *respondeat pastores: Infantem vidimus, pannis involutum, et choros angelorum laudantes Salvatorem.* It is only then that the psalm *Laudate* is sung. The contents of these two antiphons, condensed into one, make up the third response to Christmas Matins.[23]

If the only available testimony of a dramatized Portuguese liturgy is this Nativity antiphon, should it not be surmised that it was this particular presentation in which the shepherd figured, the most popular, hence the most widely disseminated? If so, this popularity would explain the predilection for the Nativity scene demonstrated by all early Peninsular playwrights.

It is in the charters decreed by the archbishop, D. Luis Pires, at the synod held in Oporto in 1477, that specific reference is found of a liturgical drama during Christmas holidays. In the section alluding to Christmas, the archbishop stipulates that:

> Não cantem chanceletas nem outras cantigas algumas, nem façam jogos no coro na igreja, salvo se for alguma boa e devota representação como

é a do Presépio ou dos reis magos, ou outras semelhantes a elas, as quais façam com toda a honestidade e devoção e sem riso nem outra turvação.[24]

The reason for this indirect and late reference lies in the fact that Church legislation is understandably more concerned with curtailing the bad than with stressing the good. The Church must have seen itself as fighting a last-ditch battle against the profane dramatic elements that threatened to overwhelm the liturgical rites.

The Secular Drama

Alongside the liturgical medieval pieces, profane representations thrived in both Spain and Portugal. The eventual merging of the two complementary currents facilitated the compositions that gave birth to modern drama. Given the nature of the secular pieces, it is not surprising that no texts containing their spoken content survive. The oral tradition of which these pieces were a part was constantly transforming their content as a result of the players' improvisation. Consequently, the actual dialogues or monologues were not recorded. What do remain, however, are references to and accounts of their productions in medieval documents. In the following pages these representations will be defined and exemplified to provide a basic appreciation of the scenario the liturgical shepherd faced as he abandoned the confines of the Church and awaited his theatrical debut.

The Latin *mimi*, as previously mentioned, did not entirely disappear after the fall of Rome. It was in these nomadic artists that traces of a defunct Roman Comedy were preserved in attenuated form. The *joculatores* or *remedadores*, as these actors were known, carried on the comic tradition in a strictly oral fashion. In a document dating from the year 1116 mention is made of *juglares* in Spain.[25] A century later, Alphonse the Wise alludes negatively to these roving entertainers in his decrees. It may be inferred that before the twelfth century no place was off-limits to them: the streets, private residences, the court, even churches and monasteries. Their performances in and around the latter so scandalized the clergy that ineffectual measures were taken to curtail the lascivious presentations known in Portuguese as *jogos* and in Spanish as *juegos*.

J. P. Wickersham Crawford, in his early but valuable study *The Spanish Pastoral Drama*, furnishes an excellent description of this medieval player:

On holidays and at weddings, his presence was indispensable, and he even occasionally entered the churches to ply his profession. His accomplishments consisted in singing, playing musical instruments, exhibiting trained animals, astonishing the gaping rustics with acrobatic feats, and sometimes in performing plays. Of the latter we know nothing, save what we may glean from the earliest religious and secular texts. Their performances were often improvised and no one dreamed of preserving their *mimicae ineptiae* and more highly developed plays.[26]

The plays to which Crawford refers are known as *arremedilhos* in Portuguese (*arremidila* in Latin; *remedillos* in Spanish), translated as "short farces" in English. In the *Cantigas de Santa Maria* of Alphonse the Wise, the term *remedillo* appears in one of the *cantigas*, leading Menéndez Pidal to define it as "el espectáculo que daba el remedador."[27] Yet it is in Portugal that the denomination first appears in connection with *mimi*. A letter from 1193, confirming the bestowal of a parcel of land on the *jogral* Bonamis and his brother Acompaniado by Sancho I, promises the monarch an *arremedilho* for his kind donation: "nos mimi supranominati debemus Domino Nostro Regi pro reboratione unum arremidilum."[28]

What, then, was this type of performance that afforded such pleasure and aroused the admiration and magnanimity of a king? It is quite likely that it possessed sufficient dramatic elements and duration to give the actors the opportunity of demonstrating their talents and originality. Certainly this *arremedilho*, as the label indicates, encompassed a single burlesque situation in which exaggerated imitation of the gestures and speech of social stereotypes (nobles, clergy, rustics, etc.), was used to improvise a hilarious scene. These situations or skits could not possibly have been limited to the ridiculing imitation of someone's features, as Luciana Stegagno Picchio has determined.[29] Had this been the case, the noun *arremidilum* would have been employed in its plural form, *arremidila*, and the mockery could not have been of any significant duration or required the participation of more than one *mimus*. The presence of more than one *mimus* implies a dialogical performance. On the other hand, if such performance was silent, the plural indicates at the very least an exchange of sorts (action-reaction); this is fundamental to drama.

If, then, these *arremedilhos* were genuine performances, what social classes or individuals did they most often satirize? Óscar de Pratt postulates that one favorite target was the legendary figures that gave rise to chivalric novels. In his opinion, these warlike characters logically made the best subjects for the art of mimicry because the courtly spectators who frequented the entertainments were themselves warlike.[30]   Nonetheless, certain prevailing social types must also have been parodied by these comic actors or authors (a term that applies since they must constantly rely on improvisation). These target-types had to comprise those professions or roles with which not only members of the court but also the common people were well acquainted. It was with this group, the humble, that the actors lived and for which it performed when their talents were not required in more lucrative venues. What, then, was one of the most logical points of contact for social groups completely isolated from each other by strictly observed medieval class codes? The local centers of worship, of course. Within their walls everyone, regardless of status, gathered to worship and expiate his or her sins.

All citizens therefore were thoroughly familiar with the solemnity and rigidity of ecclesiastical functions. It was the rigidity, in Henri Bergson's view, that lent itself to mimicking and ridicule because comedy is incapable of eliciting laughter from a flexible situation. A flexible fault is more difficult to ridicule than a rigid virtue.[31]   By flexible, we must understand a fault that is likely to touch our emotions with its pathetic potential, e.g., a drunk beating his wife. In such a situation, we may find the ramblings and personal appearance of the drunk hilarious, but our probable empathy with the victimized spouse suppresses the desire to laugh: this vitiates the comedic quality of the scene.

Let us examine hypothetically the participation of the shepherd in medieval religious ceremonies: priests impersonating shepherds paraded to the altar at Christmas Lauds, where they sang an antiphonal dialogue with the choir in Latin; the shepherds either remained at the altar until the service was concluded or retired after having sung their corresponding lines. What can we infer from this? That the shepherd was a musical supernumerary used to accentuate the "mystery" of Christ's humble birth, a role so lacking in realistic human behavior that it even expressed itself in sterile and ceremonial Church Latin. The audience's indifference stemming from its failure to establish any rapport with the religiously rigid shepherd afforded the *mimi* the opportunity to adapt the role to their lampooning *arremedilhos*.   The success of such performances compelled the Church to relax its traditional attitude and allow certain modifications in the liturgical pieces; hence the justification for the presence of dancing shepherds singing in the vernacular in the aforementioned descriptions of actual presentations. It was the mimes, supposedly unable to limit themselves to cerebral presentation, who endowed the ceremony with the vitality that was their professional concern.[32]

With the introduction of Gutenberg's invention and the subsequent dissemination of written matter, the popularity of the *arremedilho* decreased substantially because its improvisational nature could not compete with the quickly emerging theatrical compositions. However, this oral form nonetheless left its indelible mark in the evolution of Iberian drama.

During the early fifteenth century another form of entertainment evolved from the *arremedilho*; unlike its progenitor, it was performed strictly for the aristocracy. In the *momo*, as this new spectacle came to be known, members of the court took part, and there were instances when the king himself was included. This does not mean that the *vulgus* was excluded, for in 1451 and in 1490 people from all walks of life attended the anniversary celebrations of the marriage of Princess D. Leonor to Emperor Frederick III of Germany and of Prince D. Afonso to D. Isabel of Castile.

Before becoming synonymous with the spectacle, the term *momo* was applied to a masked player or to the mask he wore as the *momum quadratum* willed by the Portuguese princess D. Malfada who died in 1256 to her brother D. Pedro seems to indicate.

In Portugal, there appears to be little difference between this courtly presentation and the "pageantry associated with the word *entremés*."[33] This indicates that the Portuguese *momo* conserved the mimicry and merrymaking of the *arremedilho* just as did its neighbor but incorporated the pomposity and artifices of those pageants regarded as *entremeses* by the Castilians. Óscar de Pratt maintains that at times the Portuguese did make a distinction, but these subtleties are of little importance for the purpose of this chapter.[34]

Luiz Francisco Rebello gives a sound explanation of the compass of these shows and lists some of the European countries in which they were popular:

os "momos", divertimentos corteses em que tomavam parte fidalgos, pajens e por vezes até o próprio monarca, encenados por ocasião de festividades régias e que extraíam os seus temas das novelas de cavalaria, cujos episódios e personagens teatralmente transpunham mediante uma acção mimada, dançada e eventualmente recitada. É certo que não se trata de um género especificamente português (recordem-se, em paralelo, os *momes* franceses, as fautosas *momarie* venezianas, os *momos* castelhanos a que aludem a *Crónica de Juan II* e a *Relación* do Condestável Miguel Lucas ou o *Breve Tratado para unos momos que hizo Gómez Manrique*, em 1467); mas vários documentos contemporâneos dão-nos fiel testemunho do esplendor e da magnificência dos momos que, durante todo o século XV e nos primórdios do século XVI, se representavam na corte lusitana. As suas origens, porém, remontam ao século XIV: na

Crónica de D. João I, Fernão Lopes descreve os "vários e luzidos jogos" celebrados em 1387, no banquete nupcial do rei da Boa Memória.[35]

Momos had very little direct impact on the development of early Iberian theater. It is highly improbable that the courtiers involved would have impersonated individuals of a much lower social standing such as the shepherds who constituted the main characters in the early pieces. Participants took on mythological, allegorical, or other lofty roles in keeping with their aristocratic status. Indirectly, however, the impact of the *momo* was extremely important, since it not only aroused enough interest and financial backing for the founding of a court theater but was also the first secular representation to be transcribed.

Before concluding this discussion of the *momo*, two instances should be noted in which the shepherd is mentioned in connection with this mode of entertainment. In the first, *momo* must be understood as the masked player from whom the form later took its generic name. In the second, the shepherd's participation is not in the *momo* but in an independent religious presentation.

In discussing the origins of the *momo*, Shergold makes an interesting observation about the influence of the mummer on the actions of the shepherd in the early plays. He cites the pagan *Saturnalia* and the Christmas *Ludi* as possible sources of the *momo* and, after pointing out that these masked figures danced, brought gifts, and even played dice at the altar, theorizes as follows:

In Spain we have already seen that the Christmas *Ludi* was [sic] widely celebrated, and it may perhaps be of some interest to note that at Christmas 1464 Miguel Lucas played dice with prominent citizens of Jaen. This, however, is not associated directly with the "momos" though, as we have seen, they appeared on St. Stephen's and Innocent's Day. There are, to the best of my knowledge, no reference to dice-playing mummers in Spain, though in the Christmas plays of Encina and Gil Vicente the shepherds in the fields sometimes play games of various kinds, perhaps an echo of this dice-playing tradition.[36]

Ochoa de Ysásaga, Spanish ambassador to Portugal, described in a letter to the Catholic monarchs the *momos* held in the Portuguese court on Christmas Day of the year 1500. On Christmas Eve, the letter states, the Portuguese monarchs, D. Manuel and D. Maria, "ouviram as matinas solenemente, com órgãos, chançonetas, e pastores, que na devida altura entraram na capela dançando e cantando gloria in excelsis Deo."[37]

In sum, it is safe to say that the first theatrical character, the shepherd, owed its origin to the religious drama's need for static, subordinate figures with which to stage its didactic "mysteries." The rigidity imposed on this figure by its limited, perfunctory role lent itself to ridicule in the secular oral drama that thrived outside the church walls. After the *momo*, the founding of a court theater and the recording and dissemination of popular plays by the printing press, both Portuguese and Spanish drama evolved at giant strides.

It must be observed, nevertheless, that for both the Iberian Peninsula and the rest of Western Europe, secular dramatic tendencies in no way presuppose a religious drama. After all, were not parishioners and clergy alike descendants of those pagans who roared with laughter when the *mimi*, with no ill intent, jeered at the ancient gods? As John E. Keller puts it:

> This form of drama, the theatre of mimes, survived from the classical period through the so-called Dark Ages into medieval and Renaissance Europe, surely including Spain. And some varieties of such drama, read or recited by the narrator, added original touches. Some mimes did not continue the age-old silent form of theatrical presentation: they began to speak or sing their parts.[38]

All that counteracted the seriousness and formality of the existing order (e.g., the medieval religious parodies, the dancing in the temples) has its roots in pre-Roman folk humor. This humor, entering literary circles in the apotheosis of Greek literature, was subsequently inherited by the Romans. With the advent of the Middle Ages, the corpus of classical literature went largely ignored; yet the festive, mocking spirit of the folk maintained its comic elements in the carnival processions and pageants of the era. This accounts for what Bakhtin labels the carnival attitude toward the world, an attitude found in the early Peninsular plays and the ones that followed. We will now turn to the examination of these observations in the following chapter.

2
The Serio-Comic Genres: A Brief Overview

In the preceding pages we observed that insufficient historical data concerning the origins of Iberian drama preclude any authoritative conclusion; we now direct our attention to what appears to be Gil Vicente's generic sources in the hope that such examination may lend support to his inclusion among the continuators of Western literary tradition.

In this chapter, the description of the serio-comic characteristics in the Old Attic Comedy and Menippean satire (a type of satire where the idea or world view supplants plot considerations) bears a striking similarity to description of Gil Vicente's dramatic genre. Actually, the characteristics that Bakhtin sees as essential to Menippean satire can be found, with certain alterations, in Gil Vicente. It must not be inferred that Master Gil possessed a firsthand knowledge of ancient literature even though Eugenio Asensio, Stephen Reckert, and Américo da Costa Ramalho so argue. It is the author's view that, despite their sound research, their arguments are inconclusive. He therefore supports Michaëlis de Vasconcelos's contention that Vicente's erudition was essentially limited to the religious literature of the Middle Ages and to Spanish and Portuguese writers of the time. As was already stated, much of his early inspiration was drawn from the plays of the Spanish primitives.[1]

However, even in the scanty and limited dramatic sources the impact of the social interaction of carnival (informal dialogue), on which the Menippean satire and other serio-comic genres base their universal view, was felt. In Christian literature, this impact stemmed from two sources: the ancient Christian literary tradition in which elements of the Menippean satire thrived, and the powerful, direct influence of the medieval carnival. The secular writer, on the other hand, was influenced by the religious pieces and/or by carnival itself.

Although any literary genre perforce undergoes multiple alterations from its inception in order to stay abreast of the ever-changing demands of its milieu, its fundamental elements persist. Such elements, of course, do not remain static; only through regular renewal—that is, contemporization—are they able to endure. However, upon close examination the archaic elements of any genre can be discerned, thus revealing the source(s). As Bakhtin puts it:

> A genre lives in the present but always *remembers* its past, its beginnings. Genre is a representative of creative memory in the process of literary development. Precisely for this reason genre is capable of guaranteeing the *unity* and *uninterrupted continuity* of this development. (*Dostoevsky*, 106)

Let us now turn to the origin and development of the ancient serio-comic sources that imparted to the Vicentine comedy its generic characteristics.

Carnival and the Carnivalization of Literature

The culture of folk humor excercised an enormous impact on both Middle Ages and Renaissance. In the medieval period, carnival pageants and comic shows of the marketplace provided an opportunity for collective venting of the innate humor of the people. In these spectacles, the culture of folk-carnival humor constructed a world at a moral and social remove from the prescribed formal order of the ecclesiastical and feudal society. Public laughter became institutionalized in the carnival (here signifying the conglomeration of festivals, rites, and forms of a carnival type), its therapeutic function generally acknowledged by an elite that perceived it as a safety valve for the frustrations of a rigidly stratified society.

In the ephemeral, unreal world of carnival, all social barriers were lifted, creating a situation in which the entire population commingled in the illusion of a classless society. This festive interlude benefited both the downtrodden who were afforded the chance to deride an establishment that denied them vertical mobility, and the aristocratic and clerical hierarchy, who could enjoy themselves in the irresponsible, carefree—albeit short-lived—atmosphere of revelry. The elites achieved this freedom by temporarily forsaking the rigid formalities that buttressed their power throughout the nonfestive months.

The seasonal freedom provided by carnival yielded a renewal of life, a chance to sample a society without restrictions and the untrammeled liberties that in a non-carnival setting would have led to anarchy. Bakhtin defines the participatory nature of carnival as follows:

> Carnival is not a spectacle seen by the people; they live in it, and everyone participates because its very idea embraces all people. While carnival lasts, there is no other life outside it. During carnival time life is subject only to its laws, that is, the laws of its own freedom. It has a universal spirit; it is a special condition of the entire world, of the world's revival and renewal, in which all take part. Such is the essence of carnival, vividly felt by all its participants. (*Rabelais*, 7-8)

The temporary abrogation of hierarchic boundaries—i.e., the powerful coming in contact with the weak, the religious with the skeptic, the learned with the illiterate, the craftman with the peasant —produced a new system of relations. The protocol, prejudices, and values of noncarnival life yielded to a festival mingling, to familiar and informal contact that ordinarily would have been unacceptable. This manifest kinship operated at a well-defined level of sensuality that possessed its own codes and sets of expectations. It created the *mésalliances* so typical of carnival life. During carnival season, a topsy-turvy world sprang into being, un *monde à l'envers*, by the relaxation or inversion of hierarchy and the unfettered interaction of merrymakers in the carnival square.

Antecedents of the medieval carnival culture can be seen in the pagan rites of the Indo-European peoples. The term *carnival* may have arisen with the beginnings of Christianity, but its distinguishing characteristics date from time immemorial. Primitive societies the world over have celebrated the passing of the seasons and its effect on agriculture. In these celebrations, laughter played an eminent role because it enhanced the festive mood. This laughter, stemming from the very core of carnival, was not directed at any particular group or situation but at life as a whole, at everyone, including the very individuals who engendered it, for they too formed part of the oneness of life. To have been excluded, not to have been able to laugh at oneself, would have defeated the purpose of carnival laughter, depriving the reveler of the revitalizing function of carnival and reducing him to a modern satirist who arrogates to himself a position above his targets and therefore remedies nothing. Not to understand the ambivalent nature of medieval carnival laughter is to misapprehend the mentality of pre-eighteenth-century man. The eighteenth century has here been chosen as a dividing line between two eras, in agreement with Bakhtin's observation:

> Until the second half of the seventeenth century, people were *direct participants* in carnival acts and in a carnival sense of the world; they still *lived* in carnival, that is, carnival was one of the forms of life itself. Therefore carnivalization was experienced as something unmediated (several genres in fact directly serviced carnival). *The source of carnivalization was carnival itself.* In addition, carnivalization had a genre-shaping significance; that is, it determined not only the content but also the very generic foundations of a work. From the second half of the seventeenth century, carnival almost completely ceases to be a direct source of carnivalization, ceding its place to the influence of already carnivalized literature; in this way carnivalization becomes a purely literary tradition. (*Dostoevsky*, 131).

In origin, carnival was a plowing and sowing festival, forming part of the public cult designed to assure successful crops. That the Roman Saturnalia came to be held near year's end (17 December) seems incongruent with the very nature of carnival, though it may have been related to the winter solstice. Whatever the reasons, one fact stands out: the peoples living under Roman rule extended this festival by degrees until it coincided with the plowing season.

Carnival, by definition, is a syncretic pageant form ritualistic in nature. This form is subject to modifications depending on the era, peoples, and the particular festivals. For carnival to create the classless society that it envisioned for its celebration, it must adopt new means of communication. The language and gestures of ordinary life must be modified; otherwise social stratification would have obviated the carnival atmosphere. The speech and gestures of the marketplace, because of their uninhibiting, pragmatic, and direct nature, lent themselves to the bridging of the communication gap.

In the marketplace, individuals dealt with each other on an even footing. For example, a customer would approach a vendor or a fellow buyer and strike up a friendly conversation; formalities were eschewed and the dialogue assumed an air of familiarity: physical contact such as a pat on the back or a slight nudge was common; obscene words and piquant remarks salted the exchange; reciprocal derision might or might not occur, depending on the length of the conversation and the nature of the parties involved.

None of these familiarities per se entailed any element of laughter, but since they stood at the antipode of formality and seriousness, they acquired in carnival the accoutrements of laughter and became ambivalent. This type of communication transcended mere verbal exchange to encompass a rather complex amalgam of symbols, gestures, and attitudes that, along with utterances, led to the sensuous, ambivalent, serio-comical language of carnival. It was shaped both by isolated personal gestures within the festivities and by the complicated ritual of the mass.

The dialogical and sensuous nature of the carnival idiom that took shape and endured over many centuries found immortality in serio-comic literature. The term itself is appropriately ambivalent, befitting carnival. According to Bakhtin:

> this [carnival] language cannot be translated in any full or adequate way into a verbal language, and much less into a language of abstract concepts, but it is amenable to a certain transposition into a language of artistic images that has something in common with its concretely sensuous nature; that is, it can be transposed into the language of literature. (*Dostoevsky*, 122)

Yet the carnivalization of literature must not be seen as a medieval phenomenon. It dates back to the birth of Greek comedy and the emergence of satire (Menippus) as it supplanted the Socratic dialogues. The rise of comedy in the late Middle Ages (Gil Vicente's period), after classical comedy had fallen into oblivion, must be attributed to the same factor that gave rise to classic comedy: the ever-present humor in the folk rituals and festivities. We shall return to the carnivalization of classical literature later in this chapter.

One of the most adaptable qualities of carnival was the familiarity that it fostered. By transposing this familiarity to his production, the author was conceiving a genre that would become the antithesis of the epic and the tragedy. Both carnival and the carnivalization of literature combated all that was formal and serious. This is most evident in the structuring of plot and the resulting situations. Whereas in serious fiction (higher genres), the author goes unnoticed as the characters develop the rigid plot, in comic fiction the author is sensed as omnipresent since the characters serve as mouthpieces to relay his personal grievances. This produces a familiarity between author and characters inconceivable in higher genres. Familiarity also facilitated the logic of *mésalliances* and debasement (profanities) that altered literary verbal style. Consequently, comic literature in both antiquity and the Middle Ages reflected the frivolity associated with popular celebrations, employing the latter's forms and symbols. The history of comedy as a recognized literary genre may be viewed as the "effort to bring back those original popular celebrations where worship of natural forces and a esprit of individualism and anarchy were manifested."[2] We shall now attempt to demonstrate the aspects that define the carnival attitude incorporated into serio-comic literature.

The mock crowning and inevitable discrowning of the carnival king is the main event of the festivity. In one form or another this ritual is universal in carnival-type festivals. The act makes manifest the carnival world view: the pathos of vicissitudes and changes, of death and renewal. Crowning and discrowning are entirely congruent with the origin of carnival, for spring presupposes winter (the agricultural seasons versus the nonagricultural), while poverty and ill health presuppose salvation and eternal glory. Perhaps the best example in Western literature is chapter LIII of Cervantes's *Don Quixote*, where, having served as a governor of the island of Barataria, Sancho Panza, is forced to resign the post, incapable of enduring the responsibilities and hardships that attend power. Here, then, we find a clear instance of the crowning/discrowning motif applied to literature. If we accept this concept, then the intent of the opening lines of chapter LIII is quite evident:

> To imagine that things in this life are always to remain as they are is to indulge in an idle dream. It would appear, rather, that everything moves in a circle, that is to say, around and around: springs follows summer, summer the harvest season, harvest autumn, autumn winter, and winter spring; and thus does time continue to turn like a never-ceasing wheel. Human life alone hastens onward to its end, swifter than time's self and without hope of renewal, unless it be in that other life that has no bounds.[3]

As stated by Samuel Putnam, the meaning of this passage has occasioned a lively controversy among editors and commentators, and several emendations have been made. Putnam shares with Alexander Duffield the impression that Cervantes's intention was probably humorous, a desire to poke fun at the "Mohammedan philosopher," Cid Hamete.[4]

Later in the chapter, Sancho, preparing to leave the island, declares: "Clear the way, gentlemen, and let me go back to my old freedom. Let me go look for my past life so that I may be resurrected from this present death."[5] It was this positive attitude that pervaded the act of discrowning in carnival: discrowning (death) was not interpreted as destructive or finalizing but as a creative or resuscitative ritual. The seasons do not cease with the end of winter; rather spring comes. Similarly, time does not come to a standstill with the last day of the year; a new year begins. Carnival must not be interpreted to celebrate that which is replaced, but as the very act of replaceability. It knows no absolutes, only the joyous relativity of everything on this planet, which from its very inception is ambivalent. Without this ambivalence, change could not occur and neither could life. This is why the ritual of discrowning was most often transferred to the literary sphere to aid, in particular, plot development. Nevertheless, discrowning must not be separated from crowning, for this would lead to a loss of significance within carnival and *belles-lettres* alike.

Parody, which characterized much of the literature of antiquity and the Middle Ages, is another key aspect of carnival. Since the object of carnival is derision of the formal, structured world, it stands to reason that through parodic presentations of such a world ritual laughter (its objective) could be attained. In life, everything in the serious realm of experience has its comic double, a fact that should not imply that parody negates or poses a threat to that which it satirizes. On the contrary, it renews its target and strengthens its position within the system; parody is successful only when its object (the formal) is institutionalized, deeply imbedded in society, and familiar to its members. For this reason, the ancients did not oppose parody of the status quo, and this tolerant attitude endured through the Renaissance. In parody, as in discrowning, the subject apparently dies or is destroyed only to be reborn in the manner of the mythical phoenix.

Parody was therefore highly representative of the carnivalized forms of literature. In the *Libro de buen amor* of Juan Ruiz, Archpriest of Hita, we find many such examples along with the carnival atmosphere associated with the genre. One example is the humorous debate between an ignorant Roman knave and a wise Greek doctor. Though both the Roman and the Greek wore the robes of a learned man, the former was an acknowledged fool, whereas the latter was a genuine sage:

> They dressed him out in richest clothes, in pomp and circumstance
> As Doctor of Philosophy of great significance.
> Upon a chair he sat and said with stupid arrogance:
> "Okay now, all you Greeks with learned arguments, advance."
>
> A Greek moved forward then, a doctor polished, logical,
> The chosen one of every Greek and praised among them all.
> He mounted to the other chair, when all were gathered there,
> And as agreed, they started making signs across the hall.[6]

First of all, this is a carnival *mésalliance* in that two individuals, intellectually opposite, come into contact and deal with each other on an equal basis. Second, the atmosphere is that of the carnival square—the place where carnival performances customarily took place—since we find that "all were gathered there." Third, university knowledge and speech are masterfully parodied, for not only did the uneducated knave win the day for Rome, but also, unknowingly, he was able to make effective use of the *signs* employed by learned men. As mentioned earlier, parody does not attempt to do away with existing institutions. Had this been the case, Spanish universities would have declined in number during the latter part of the fourteenth century, and we know this not to be the case.

The Old Attic Comedy

Suzana Camargo unduly censures Bakhtin for having neglected the importance of the Attic Comedy in the development of the Menippean satire when she alleges that "o teórico russo, em suas considerações sobre as origens da sátira menipea, parece não levar a influência da comédia ática na formação daquela."[7] This is somewhat unjust; although Bakhtin did not elaborate on such influence, he clearly states that "in the ancient period, early Attic comedy and the entire realm of the serio-comical was subjected to a particularly powerful carnivalization" (*Dostoevsky*, 129). True, this statement does not directly link the Attic (= Old) Comedy to the Menippean satire, but if we take into consideration that the latter was a result of the carnivalization of literature, it must be logically deduced that Attic Comedy perforce played an influential role.

With regard to the Socratic dialogue from which the Menippean satire took many of its traits, mainly its dialogical nature, Bakhtin points out that "this carnival base also brings Socratic dialogue close in several respects to the agons of ancient Attic comedy" (*Dostoevsky*, 132). Therefore, it is imperative to analyze, even summarily, the earliest form of carnival drama of which examples have survived. Such analysis assumes added importance in this study since comic drama forms the bulk of Gil Vicente's work.

"Old Comedy" was the comedy staged in Athens during the fifth century B.C. Its very origins, like those of tragedy, are impossible to trace owing to the scarcity of surviving material. Through the sparse extant literature and ceramic pieces that have been excavated, we know that in Attica, both in Athens and in the small towns and villages, a religious procession known as *komos* was observed. Its participants were not actors but volunteers who danced and sang merrily while wearing masks and costumes representing various animals. The masks and costumes were worn to conceal identity and had no dramatic purpose. The leaders of these dances or processions were known as *phallophoroi* or phallus-carriers because they bore large poles (*phalloi*), symbols of the male organ. While parading, they directed abusive comments at bystanders and shouted obscene jokes.

This entire performance was held in honor of the fertility gods, especially Dionysus, who in addition to being the god of wine was also a fertility deity; he was linked in the popular mind with the birth and rebirth that the ever-changing seasons bring about because he, as a god, had undergone death and rebirth.

That Dionysus was also the god of wine explains the large amounts of this beverage imbibed by the phallus-carriers to reach the delirium that gave rise to the desired lewd behavior. It may be reasonably deduced that this wild frolic possessed all the hallmarks of an ancient "carnival": it was a religious celebration in honor of the fertility gods (death/rebirth); it featured the invectives and obscenity of the marketplace; it suspended the hierarchical order to invoke therapeutic disorder.

Alexis Salomos, after describing the events of Dionysiac festivals, gives an excellent account of what he considers the therapeutic function of these festivities:

> Was not this, after all, the ultimate social purpose of the Dionysiac festivals: to provide an organized and controlled outlet for man's punitive impulses? By instituting on religious pretexts a well-scheduled orgy, the state let men run wild in the streets and fields, free to masquerade, to get drunk, to make love, to exhaust their muscles in dance and their vocal chords in song, in other words, to spend all their resources and energy—lust or madness—during those fixed days, so that during the rest of the year they could calmly and patiently attend to their daily work. Dionysiac festivals were an indispensable emergency exit to man's primitive urges; they were also a counter-balance to the exasperating dullness of his everyday life.[8]

Could we not apply this rationale to the Christian carnivals that so typified the Middle Ages?

It is believed that the comic chorus, as it is known to us, sprang from the primitive *komos*: as the revelers heaped insults on the crowd during their frantic parade, it responded in kind, and this reciprocal banter became the antiphonal song of the chorus. There were other influences on comedy: the animal disguises, musical instruments, singing and dancing, spectacular and ceremonial events, and the overall orgiastic character. All these elements are found in Old Comedy, of which Aristophanes' plays are the only surviving representatives, the only works remaining in their entirety. However, there are other elements in these plays that must be attributed to another type of performance.

The Dorians of Megara were distinguished by a peculiar fondness for jest and ridicule, and produced farcical entertainers full of jovial merriment and rude jokes.[9] During the Dionysian festival, the actors of the Dorian farce wore comic human masks (a drunkard's face) and the phallos somewhat resembling the Attic players. In addition, they padded their stomachs and buttocks to stress the lower areas of the body. Their act consisted in parodying scenes from everyday life along with mythical and heroic figures. From their daily-life parodies, many stock characters are known: the fruit stealer, the foreign doctor, the gallant, the bawd, and the drunkard whose figure later reappeared in Old Comedy. Of these dramas, no fragment has reached us; knowledge of their content has been through the writings of Plutarch and Athenaeus.[10]

Epicharmus, a native of Cos, who spent some time in Megara before finally emigrating to Syracuse, appears to have been the first to adjust the stock characters of the Dorian farce to well-organized plots and elaborate dialogues.[11] He achieved this by fusing the refined recitative poetry of the Ionians with the rude farcical elements of the Dorians, thus giving the coarse, disconnected Doric farce an artistic and literary form.

His comedies may be divided into three categories:

(a) Mythological travesties, burlesque versions of stories about heroes or gods: Dionysus, Odysseus, and especially Heracles, whose adventures and gluttony provided such copious material for later playwrights.

(b) Social comedies—the portraiture of contemporary life and character—in which the parasite, the drunk, the boor, the boastful soldier, were extracted from the popular Doric farce, and transposed into the literary realm.

(c) Presentations of conflict, not of opposing characters or types, but of nonhuman entities or abstractions: a duel between personifications, like the contention of Earth and Sea, Logos and Logina, etc.[12]

In Epicharmus we find the earliest example of the carnivalization of literature because the characters and situations belonged to the Bacchic festivities and their serio-comic (religious/profane) core. Yet, once composed, the comedies bore no relation to the ancient Dionysiac carnival.

Whereas Attic Comedy appears to owe much to Epicharmus, it must not be surmised that the former was the end result of the latter. As previously seen, the origin of Attic Comedy can be undeniably traced to the *komos*; by 486 B.C., when the archon granted the dramatists a chorus with actors rather than with volunteers, comedy was officially recognized as an established art form and incorporated into the Great Dionysia, the birthplace of tragedy. Alexis Salomos has commented concerning the differences between Epicharmus and Attic Comedy:

> Sicilian dramaturgy, as elaborated by Epicharmus (the playwright produced his plays while living in Syracuse), differed radically from the Athenian. Its plays were neither as lyrical nor as spectacular. They lacked the Dionysiac flavor which linked comedy to public festivity. *They hardly touched political topics or mentioned real people* [italics mine]. They did not thrust violent messages before the public. And most significant of all, the "comic chorus" was something they completely ignored.[13]

In her study, Suzana Camargo, after stressing the influential importance of Attic Comedy on Menippean satire, discusses at some length the impact of Epicharmus's drama on the Attic Comedy, pointing out that in Epicharmus one finds three principal traits associated with Attic Comedy. The last of these is unusual for Camargo states that Epicharmus's comedy "não se limita à sátira genérica, descendo à sátira pessoal em tom de paródia, o que faria que a comédia ática fosse mais tarde censurada oficialmente."[14] This is a contention with which many scholars would disagree. The scholarly works consulted for this study unanimously affirmed that Epicharmus's attacks or satires were never directed at any particular individual—a view the author shares. In the quotation above, Salomos unequivocally expresses the opposing view in the italicized sentence.[15]

For the present study, however, it is of no consequence whether Camargo or the classical scholars are correct. From the extant fragments of Epicharmus, it is impossible to determine the exact contents of their corresponding plays. There is even the possibility that the plays were not staged but simply composed for reading.

What does matter is the fact that Epicharmus was as well known as a philosopher as he was a dramatist. As C. M. Bowra puts it: "He [Epicharmus] liked both parodies and philosophical discussions and, if he really was the first to compose plays in this way, he is rightly regarded as the father of comedy."[16] The blend of the serious (philosophy) with the comic (parody) characterizes all carnivalized literature. Bakhtin, though he understood the importance of Attic Comedy in the formation of carnivalized literature, excludes it from this category in listing the genres the ancients termed serio-comic. Where he obtained this information he does not say, but he goes on to add that "the ancients themselves distinctly sensed its [serio-comical] fundamental uniqueness and counterposed it to the serious genres—the epic, the tragedy, the history, classical rhetoric, and the like" (*Dostoevsky*, 107).

Certainly, neither the works of Epicharmus nor those of Aristophanes are easily accomodated in any of the serious genres; both wrote a type of comedy that unmistakably belongs to and stems from carnival. How, then, are we to prove that Aristophanic comedy (Old Attic Comedy) is rightly part of the serio-comical? It is insufficient to allege that simply because comedy originated in ancient Greece from Dionysiac festivities we have a carnivalized genre that accordingly belongs to the serio-comical.

Bakhtin offers three external characteristics of the serio-comical that he sees as a result of the transformational character of the carnival attitude:

(a) The focus of the serio-comic genres, their starting point for understanding, evaluating, and formulating reality is the *present*, often the topicality of the immediate present.

(b) The serio-comic genres are not based on *legend* and do not elucidate themselves by means of the legend—they are *consciously* based on *experience* and on *free imagination*; their relationship to legend is in most cases deeply critical, and at times displays the cynicism nature of the exposé.

(c) The serio-comic genres reject the stylistic unity of the epic, the tragedy, lofty rhetoric, and the lyric. They are typified by multiplicity of tone in a story and a mixture of the high and low, the serious and the comic.

Before applying these criteria to Aristophanes' work, let us now note some of Lawrence Giangrande's remarks on Aristophanes and the serio-comical:

> Whereas his contemporaries depart from the imaginative and aesthetic to the point of slighting the laughable (*geloin*) and overemphasizing the serious (*spoudaion*), Aristophanes tends to combine the two aspects in a virtually perfect balance. We must bear in mind, then, that Aristophanes was a serio-comic playwright, and that he, when buffoonery was laid aside, dealt with literary questions critically, for his world was one in which tragedy had almost a monopoly on teaching and tragedy had, to his mind, become a vehicle for the transmission of atheistic ideas, cheap cleverness, sordid realism, and the degradation of human ideals.[17]

Old Comedy, therefore, had a strong moral intent. Subject in its later days to the prohibition of personal abuse and influenced by the Epicharmian-type comedy, it prefigured the development of a balanced commingling of the serious and comic into *spoudaiogeloion*.[18] Aristophanes' *The Frogs*, the last and perhaps the finest extant specimen of Old Comedy (the *Ecclesiazusae* and *Plutus* belong to Middle Comedy), meets Bakhtin's criteria and substantiates Giangrande's comments.

In 405 B.C., when the play won first place at the Lenaean festival, the socio-political situation in Athens was quickly deteriorating. After the death of Euripides in 407 and Sophocles in 406, quality drama could no longer be composed by the second-rate playwrights who survived the two great figures. Further, political decadence and corruption were keeping pace with the literary decline. The oligarchic regime of the Four Hundred had supplanted the old democracy and after just four and a half months in power succumbed to the austere combination of oligarchy and democracy that characterized the rule of the Five Thousand. This government also failed to endure more than a few months. By 410, the former democracy had reestablished itself, and once again demagogues and servile flatterers returned to public life. Among these figured Cleophon, the new ruler, whose liberal policies depleted the state's coffers.

Alcibiades, in hopes of reconciliation with Athens, won a number of battles on its behalf but after being recalled was soon banished. In 406, promising citizenship to all slaves who would join the fleet, Cleon won a significant battle over the Spartans at Arginusae; the victory was marred, however, by Cleon's obstinacy in accepting the dubious peace proposals and the court-martial and consequent execution of six of ten generals charged with abandoning the dead and wounded to the waves.

All these distressing circumstances lent themselves to the plot development of *The Frogs*: Dionysus, along with his servant Xanthias, descends into Hades to fetch Euripides and restore him to the world of the living so that tragedy may once again thrive. After an encounter with Herakles to inquire about the best path to the nether world, Dionysus crosses the Styx on Charon's barge while Xanthias, because he is a slave, must circle the shore to get across. Once in Hades, the two men direct their steps toward Pluto's palace but are detained a few times by either friends or foes of Herakles who mistake Dionysus for the demigod. In accordance with each circumstance, Dionysus compels Xanthias to exchange costumes so that the cowardly god may either avoid misfortune or reap advantage. Finally, Aeacus, a servant of the gods, has both men flogged. Since lashes are not supposed to hurt an immortal, Aeacus is trying to determine which is the real god. When both servant and god alike cry out, Aeacus has no alternative than to lead them to Pluto, who as a god possesses the divine ability to tell them apart.

While the characters are inside Pluto's palace, the chorus takes over and recites the parabasis, which deals strictly with politics and has no bearing on the remainder of the play. Next, Aeacus and Xanthias appear commenting on the contest that is to take place between Aeschylus and Euripides to establish which is the better tragedian. Dionysus is appointed to serve as judge of the event. The contest starts and the tragedians level charges and countercharges against each other and, in so doing, produce one of the best tractates on ancient literary criticism that has survived. The outcome of the contest is decided in favor of Aeschylus, not because he is the superior poet, but because Dionysus deems him better able to offer Athens sound advice than his opponent. Immediately, Pluto allows the winning tragedian to return to the world of the living in the company of Dionysus and slave.

From this description, it is evident that the first criterion for the serio-comical is met. We have here a play entirely based on the present (that of Aristophanes); the presentation bears no relationship with the distant past, as is the case with the epic and tragedy, which tended to draw their topics from the legendary and the mythical. The present in this play is not only literary; the political present permeates the piece as well and surfaces in remarks such as the one made by Xanthias upon Dionysus's jesting insistence that the slave carry both package and ass: "What a pity I did not fight at sea; I would baste your ribs for that joke."[19] This is in reference to the sea battle at Arginusae; had the slave participated, he would be a free man and consequently his master's equal. The chorus's parabasis in the middle of the play is a direct attack on the leadership of the state and offers sound advice that must be heeded if the Polis is to survive.[20]

The second criterion, as Bakhtin affirms, is inseparably bound up with the first. Therefore, the main topics of *The Frogs* are derived from actual experience, from events witnessed by the author or that had a direct impact on his world. That the plot unfolds in an unreal setting and includes several mythological protagonists does not signify that the play is heavily dependent on legend. The depiction of the mythical beings is essentially antiheroic, deflating. In the words of Lois Spatz:

> The ridiculous figure of Dionysus himself, intimidated and outshone by his slave, mocked by Herakles for his costume, and finally beaten by

Aeacus reduces the gods themselves and the impenetrable cosmos to human and controllable dimensions.[21]

Aristophanes' use of myth forms part of the creative process: free imagination. It discredits the lofty epical and tragical figures by endowing them with the vices and weaknesses associated with the lowly human creature, e.g., Herakles' gluttony and Dionysus's cowardice. Death is stripped of its mystery and reduced to a simple continuation of life or rebirth into another reality, a reality with striking similarities to the present one. This is most evident in the section where the Dead Man, having refused the price offered him by Dionysus for carrying the god's baggage down to Hades, responds: "I would sooner go back to earth again."[22] The journey to the afterlife takes on the qualities of a journey to a neighboring city, for the Dead Man both speaks up when addressed and demands money that he hopes to use upon reaching his destination. Death in this case becomes life elsewhere; it is deprived of its tragic finality.

The less-than-final nature of death associated with the genre provides The Frogs with its unifying (though loosely-knit) structure. Dionysus, without having to resort to any of the violent means suggested by Herakles, arrives at the realm of the dead, there to serve as arbiter to two competing tragedians, and returns unscathed with the victor to his point of departure: the world of the living. In tragedy, the inflexibility identified with the afterlife would not have permitted "resuscitation" of the hero; death, considered the supreme trial for mortals, would have exhausted the hero's energies, either proving him empty or confirming his strengths.[23]

The dichotomous construction of the play meets the third criterion of the serio-comical: in the first half, Dionysus appears as a buffoon whose actions lead him from one hilarious situation to another. He typifies all the lowly instincts of mankind and is morally overshadowed by his own slave, Xanthias, whose figure, for the first time in Western literature, is presented on the same level as—and at times on a higher level than—his master; here, master and slave share the principal role.

In the second half, Dionysus ceases to be a fool and suddenly displays sagacity and wisdom. Assigned to judge the contest between Aeschylus and Euripides, his action affirms his common sense: his decision does not determine who is the better poet, but who will prove the better counselor with regard to the welfare of Athens.

Each half repels the other in style. If the first half is full of witticisms, grotesqueness, low language (in short, all the components of comedy), the second half is marked by its literary language, sententiousness, sober atmosphere, and dialectical discourse, i.e., the components of tragedy. This mixture of the seriousness of tragedy and the whimsy of comedy fulfills the third criterion.

Parodical reconstructed quotations are most common in the piece. A good example is to be found when Herakles labels as idiotic the phrases of tragedy that Dionysus finds so creative and the latter retorts, parodying Euripides: "Don't come trespassing on my mind; you have a brain of your own to keep thoughts in."[24] In Bakhtin's view, parody is an integral element in all carnivalized genres. Old Comedy owed much of its popularity to the parodying of legendary and heroic figures of tragedy. Its dependence on tragedy stems from its need for characters and topics already well known to the populace through tragedy so its own plots would not founder in incomprehension. Other characteristics further strengthen the classification of this typical play of Aristophanes as serio-comic.

The Frogs displays a bilevel construction not only of style, as mentioned above, but also of surroundings: action and dialogue are transferred from earth to Hades. In Menippean satire, a similar transference occurs with the inclusion of Olympus as well, resulting in a trilevel construction. However, it should be noted that in *The Frogs*, the original point of departure for Dionysus was Olympus because he himself was a god—in the piece, this is understood and no reference is made to the dwelling place of the gods. True, these multiple levels of action existed in tragedy also, but in *The Frogs* "the choice of Dionysus as the central quester permits the analogy between art and politics to develop on a grand scale and to include comedy as well as tragedy."[25] Certainly, this was not the function of the tragic hero.

From this multilevel construction descend the "threshold dialogues" so common in Menippean satire. These dialogues take place at the entrance of a place of difficult access. In *The Frogs*, dialogues of this nature occur twice: when Dionysus goes to Herakles' house to seek his guidance and when Dionysus and Xanthias, having arrived in Hades, attempt to see Pluto and are detained at the threshold by Aeacus. We shall return later to this subject.

The two-in-one images and *mésalliances* that stress the ambivalent nature of the serio-comical are well exhibited in the play. Herakles, answering the door and catching sight of Dionysus's motley attire, exclaims:

Oh! 'tis enough to make a fellow hold his sides to see this lion's skin over a saffron robe! What does this mean? Buskins and a bludgeon! What connection have they? Where are you off to in this rig?[26]

Aristophanes has created a visual two-in-one figure: the saffron robe and buskins were symbols of effeminacy; the lion's skin and the bludgeon characterized manliness. The sharp effeminacy/manliness contrast manifests the carnival eccentricity that elicits laughter and underscores the ambivalent nature of man. Charles Paul Segal expounds this dual characterization as follows:

Dionysus appears as the embodiment of the comic spirit seeking a stable definition of itself and its aims. His search is presented primarily through the motifs of disguise and changeability. With the assumption of a new garment comes the testing of a new identity and the beginning of a transformation of character. Here again Aristophanes is working within the bounds of a traditional theme. To disguise the protagonist as his apparent opposite is a regular *modus operandi* of Old Comedy, familiar from the remodeling of Mnesilochus as a woman in the *Thesmophoriazo-usae* of Cratinus, where the god seems to have been disguised as Paris and even as a ram.[27]

In Hades, where Dionysus repeatedly forces Xanthias to exchange disguises, a *mésalliance* (god/mortal, master/slave) that has prevailed from the outset of the play is taken one step further, for here the exchange of disguise implies more than a mere superficial visual substitution. It embodies the fundamental ritual of carnival: crowning and discrowning.

The nether world, owing to its fantastic, illusory character, facilitates the creation of a carnival-like atmosphere and all the events it entails, i.e., free familiarity, scandals and eccentricities, crownings and discrownings, etc. Hades, in effect, becomes a carnival square. Perhaps for this reason the multilevel construction enjoyed a tremendous popularity within the serio-comic genres.

Thus, when Xanthias puts on Dionysus's costume only to surrender it moments later when his master reclaims it for his own benefit, we are witnessing a literary crowning/discrowning. Dionysus, by donning his servant's outfit, has momentarily debased himself while Xanthias rises to the status of a god. In the nether world, the carnival logic of "the world turned upside down" applies; what in ordinary, everyday life would have been impossible—the exchange of social roles—occurs in the carnival atmosphere of the underworld. Still, since in carnival discrowning is inherent in the very act of coronation, Xanthias inevitably must divest himself of both the costume and short-lived ascendancy. As previously stated, the ritual of discrowning concludes the coronation and is inseparable from it. It is in the ritual of discrowning that the carnival pathos of change and renewal and the image of the creativity of death stand out in boldest clarity. Crowning/discrowning is a two-in-one ritual in which a new crowning is foreseen. Xanthias's remarks while surrendering the garments presage that his acquiescence is not conclusive: "Come then! 'tis well! take them [the garments]. But perhaps you will be needing me one day, and it please the gods."[28]

Perhaps one of the most distinctive and important qualities of serio-comic genres is the wide usage of marketplace language. Billingsgate is unavoidable in the serio-comical; it sets the carnival atmosphere and provides much of the necessary comicalness of the work. It manifests itself in the proverbs, colloquialisms, references to lowly environs and professions associated with the marketplace, oaths, abusive language, mention of the lower half of the body, etc. None of these forms of expression was originally associated with laughter, but since they were excluded from the sphere of official speech because of taboos, in the carnival atmosphere they acquired a comedic aspect and a therapeutic function.

In the scene where Dionysus, before descending into Hades, encounters Herakles, he bids from him the following:

> If I have decked myself according to your pattern, 'tis that you may tell me, in case I should need them, all about the hosts who received you, when you journeyed to Cerberus; tell me of them as well as of the harbours, the bakeries, the brothels, the drinkingshops, the fountains, the roads, the eating houses and the hostels where there are the fewest bugs.[29]

Later, having befouled himself in fear of Aeacus's threats, Dionysus rationalizes his embarassing position by saying, "A poltroon would have fallen backwards, being overcome with the fumes; as for me, I got up and moreover I wiped myself clean."[30]

These excerpts demonstrate Aristophanes' use of billingsgate to reduce Dionysus to the status of a mortal and a wretched one at that. The god's desire to learn about the base marketplace atmosphere of the nether world and his unhesitating recognition that he too was subject to the realities of his lower body would have been unthinkable in tragedy or epic poetry. Yet, as Robert Flaceliere puts it:

His [Aristophanes'] disrespectful attitude to the gods was part of the comic tradition and, in this respect, the Athenians allowed their comic poets a surprising degree of freedom, considering the number and seriousness of the charges they brought for impiety; we have seen how careful even a tragic poet like Euripides had to be. The fact is, it was only comedy which enjoyed this license, probably because it was not taken seriously.[31]

Was this not also the attitude taken toward ritual festivities?

In addition to the play's many examples of billingsgate—oaths, proverbs, colloquialisms and abusive language—there are two direct references to the marketplace itself that highlight its constant presence in the comedian's creative process: "Come, Aeschylus, no flying into a temper! discuss the question coolly; poets must not revile each other like market wenches."[32] Dionysus thus reprimands Aeschylus for the abusive language he heaps upon Euripides during the contest. Later, unable to determine which of the two is the better poet, Dionysus resorts to weighing their verses on a scale so that sheer weight may determine the outcome: "Well then, come, I am going to sell the poet's genius the same way cheese is sold in the market."[33]

One last example—perhaps the most telling—of the serio-comical intent of this play are the lines sung by the Mystic Chorus in its processional hymn to Demeter: "Grant me to say much that is funny [geloia], but also much that is serious [spoudaia]."[34] Such request succinctly illustrates what has been noted throughout, and rightfully places Aristophanes among those who composed or invented the literary mixture of jest and earnestness known as spoudaiogeloion.

In concluding this section, let us reiterate that Old Attic Comedy—the most renowned comedian of which was Aristophanes, and the only representative whose plays have survived in their entirety—was the first literary art form to incorporate carnival elements in its compositions. For that reason, it should be added to the list of ancient serio-comic genres referred to by Bakhtin. Aristophanes, like Gil Vicente centuries later, obviously wanted to make people laugh and would go to any length to achieve this end; but as an exponent of the serio-comic, he also attempted to convey a moral, didactic message. In all of his plays, his preoccupation with the impending fall of the state, the moral turpitude brought about by weak, corrupt politicians, and the ruinous condition of the arts seeps through the buffooneries and gaiety of the plot to remind the audience of the present danger and suggest positive forms of action.

The Menippean Satire

The Menippean satire, listed by Bakhtin as belonging to the serio-comic (carnivalized) genres, takes its name from the Cynic philosopher Menippus of Gadara (ca. 340 - ca. 270 B.C.) who, born a slave, bought his freedom and set up residence in the city of Thebes. Unfortunately, the fact that only a fragment of his work survives obliges an indirect approach via the literary tradition.[35]

To Bakhtin the genre originated as another serio-comic genre, the Socratic dialogue, began to decline after a brief heyday. It should not be construed, however, that the Menippean satire was the product of the disintegration of the Socratic dialogue, for its source can be directly traced to carnival folklore, the influence of which is stronger in the Menippean satire. Nevertheless, it is beyond denial that Socrates and Aristophanes were two important bridges between Homer and the Cynics since both were interested in the destiny of the common man and skirted the serio-comical.[36]

Apparently, the term *Menippean satire* was first introduced by the Roman writer Varro (116 - 27 B.C.), of whose work we have only fragmentary evidence.[37] According to Saint Jerome, Varro composed 150 books, which he entitled *Saturae Menippeae*; only 600 fragments survive. One of the signature characteristics of this brand of satire was the *prosimetrum*, a medley of prose and verse believed to have been employed in the work of the real Menippus as its structural base. (At this point, it should be emphasized that *Menippean satire*—henceforth called Menippea for brevity—as applied to Gil Vicente's work, is a designation of the essence of the genre, rather than of the specific canon of the genre as in antiquity.)

Bakhtin believed that the genre originated before Menippus and mentions its early representatives:

> the genre itself arose considerably earlier: its first representative was perhaps Anthisthenses, a pupil of Socrates and one of the authors of Socratic dialogues. Menippean satires were also written by Aristotle's contemporary Heraclides Ponticus, who, according to Cicero, was also the creator of a kindred genre, the logistoricus (a combination of the Socratic dialogue with fantastic histories). We have already an indisputable representative of the Menippean satire in Bion Borysthenes, that is, "the man from the banks of the Dniepr" (third century B.C.). Then came Menippus, who gave the genre more definite form, and then Varro, of whose satires numerous fragments have survived. (*Dostoevsky*, 113)

It is, then, their carnival origins, common to both Socratic dialogue and Menippea that classifies these genres as serio-comical. A superficial reading of certain Socratic dialogues (Plato or Xenophon) may erroneously lead the reader to assume that they belong to the genre of rhetoric. But the foundations of Socratic dialogue are essentially carnivalesque. In spite of its apparent involved literary form and profound philosophical content, its creative pivot was the carnival "debate" between the counterpoised opposites of life and death, summer and winter, light and darkness, etc. It challenged monologuist officialdom to reexamine its purported absolute truths and its monolithic seriousness, through dialectical stress on the pathos of change and joyful relativity that demolish dogma. By adopting dialogue as a truth-seeking means of discourse, the participants, regardless of social status or knowledge of the discussed topic, are forced to set aside all pretentiousness, abolish any distance between themselves and their interlocutors, and assume an attitude of familiarity toward the object of thought and truth itself. Eventually, however, towards the end of Plato's life, the monologue began to supplant the dialogue in order to embody the already formed, dogmatic *Weltanschauungen* of various philosophical schools and religious doctrines; hence, the Socratic dialogue lost all contact with the carnival world-view, becoming a simple form for expressing ready-made, indisputable truths, and degenerating finally into a question-and-answer vehicle for training neophytes, i.e., the cathechism. The Socratic dialogue eventually gave way to the Menippea, which owed a considerable debt to the former for its questioning approach to the status quo. Aristophanic comedy, as we have seen, also made its contribution.

Bakhtin classifies other writers as Menippean as well. Seneca's *Apocolocyntosis* (*The Pumpkinzation*), to which we shall return, is perhaps the best surviving example of an ancient Menippea. Allan P. Ball informs us that:

Bucheler has argued to show that in the *Apocolocyntosis* we have an example of the very kind of thing that Varro did. He recites the evident facts: that Varro was the one Roman literary model for the special kind of satire that Seneca was writing, the loosely composed skit in a mixture of prose and verse; that Varro at least once wrote such a satire on a political subject...; that many of his satires have double titles, one part Greek and the other Latin; that the scene of the *Apocolocyntosis* is in heaven, while the scenes of Varro's satires are various (and so, apparently, might include heaven); that there is the same tendency to introduce popular saws and moral reflections; that there is both the *imago antiquae et vernaculae festivitatis*; [that one finds] the frequent expressions inadmissible by *urbanitas*; the frequency of quotations from the Greek, and the general patchwork of literary allusions.[38]

Petronius's *Satyricon* has been considered a Menippea elevated almost to the status of a novel. Lucian, a Greek born in the Orient, gives in his "Menippean Satires" a notion of what the genre consisted of, albeit not in all its varieties. *The Metamorphoses* (*The Golden Ass*) of Apuleius is an extensive Menippea, though in essence rather than in structure.

The carnival element is far more evident in the Menippea than in the Socratic dialogue. Both its nucleus and its external elements manifest the total carnivalization of the genre. Certain Menippeas directly portray celebrations of a carnival type (Varro, for example, depicts Roman celebrations in two satires). According to Bakhtin, this portrayal is substantially an external or thematic connection, but it is also quite common in the Menippea. As mentioned with regard to Aristophanic comedy, the multilevels, the different planes (Olympus, the nether world, Earth) that also characterize the Menippea, call for a carnivalesque interpretation. Olympus is transformed into the carnival square where free familiarization, scandals and eccentricities, and crowning/discrowning take place. At times, scenes on Olympus entail carnival debasement or bringing-down-to-earth, as in the *Apocolocyntosis*. The nether world is a consistently carnivalized region where one finds the *mésalliances* and familiarization that occur when an emperor comes into contact with a slave, a rich man with a beggar, as in *The Frogs*; death discrowns those who wear crowns in life. The upside-down logic of carnival frequently marked the nether world: there the emperor became the slave, the slave the emperor.

The Menippea also depicts the carnivalization of earth. Streets, taverns, roads, baths, the decks of ships, accessible to individuals from all walks of life, take on the trappings of the carnival square. Scenes unfolding in such spots are portrayed realistically with their carnivalized familiar contacts, *mésalliances*, disguises and mystifications, scandals, improprieties, crownings and discrownings, etc. The *Satyricon*, also carnivalized, takes the reader from one naturalistic underworld scene to another, as does *The Golden Ass*.

The *Apocolocyntosis*, a satire on the death of emperor Claudius, meets all the requirements of the Menippea both in form and content. Indeed the Spanish-born Stoic philosopher Seneca derived many of his techniques from his predecessor Varro, but whereas the latter's *saturae* were rather good-natured, humorous exhibitions of homely philosophy intended to be popular and helpful, Seneca's satire is a direct and bitter portrayal of the ridiculous side of a dead incompetent potentate against whom the writer bore a grudge.[39] It is, as it were, a discrowning inevitably brought about by two previous coronations: Claudius, the palsied outcast, is made emperor after Caligula's assassination (first coronation); after he is poisoned by his wife Agrippina to ensure the succession of her son Nero, his apotheosis is decreed by the Senate (second coronation). In the *Apocolocyntosis*, he arrives outside the assembly of gods; after being denied divinity, he is led to the nether world (discrowning). Here we have the sameself carnival logic of an impostor's "elevation," his eventual discrowning in the carnival square (Olympus), and his downfall.

An attempt to analyze each characteristic of the Menippea in this satire is beyond the scope of this chapter.[40] Yet close scrutiny of a typical fragment illustrates several elements inherent in the serio-comic genres, elements that confirm Bakhtin's claim that their roots lie in carnival folklore.

Hercules, initially terrified by Claudius's hobble and stammer at the threshold of the gods' assembly, is reassured by the goddess Febris, who reveals Claudius's true identity. Hercules then threatens Claudius and the following ensues:

> Claudius, seeing the mighty hero, forgot his nonsense and perceived that while no one had been a match for him at Rome, here he did not have the same advantage; a cock is master only in his own dunghill. So, as well as could be made out, this is what he appeared to say: "I did hope that you, Hercules, bravest of the gods, would stand by me before the others, and if anyone had asked me who could vouch for me, I should have named you, who know me best. For if you recall, I was the one who held court before your temple [to you] all day long during the months of July and August. You know how many troubles I had there, listening to the lawyers day and night; and if you had fallen among those fellows, though you may think you are pretty courageous, you would have preferred to clean Augeas' stables. I have cleaned out much more filth. But since I want.'[41]

Claudius's speech is cut short at this point by a lacuna in the manuscript.

This excerpt from a "threshold dialogue" gives an excellent example of the literarization of the marketplace language and its use as comic relief and debasement. The frequent use of colloquialisms such as "mighty" (*valens, -ns* participles as attributive adjectives were typical of plebeian speech), "forgot his nonsense" (*oblitus nugarum,* a popular expression), "the one . . . you" (*tibi . . . tuum*, colloquial repetition), and "I had" (*contulerim*, with *con-* indicating a plebeian compound) foreshadows Claudius's fall.[42]   As the emperor senses that he no longer wields dictatorial power, his language becomes tainted by vulgarisms, a reflection of his impotence.   "A cock is master only in his own dunghill" (*Gallum in suo sterquilino plurimum posse*) has here a triple function: it is an abusive proverb belonging to the special branch of billingsgate that traces its origin to primitive communication and lends itself in the Menippea to an unrestrained carnival atmosphere; it is a pun on Claudius's Gallic origin, here employed for self-debasement; and, finally, the image of feces it contains—later repeated toward the end of the fragment—is closely related to death (Claudius is said to have given up the ghost while defecating).   Bakhtin makes some interesting comments in this respect:

> The images of feces and urine are ambivalent as are all the images of the material bodily lower stratum; they debase, destroy, regenerate, and renew simultaneously. They are blessing and humiliating at the same time. Death and death throes, labor, and childbirth are intimately interwoven. On the other hand, these images are closely linked to laughter. When death and birth are shown in their comic aspect, scatological images in various forms nearly always accompany the gay monsters created by laughter in order to replace the terror that has been defeated. For this reason, too, these images are indissolubly linked with the underworld. It can be said that excrement represents bodies and matter that are mostly comic; it is the most suitable substance for the degrading of all that is exalted. (*Rabelais*, 151-52)

Claudius's death is in fact closely linked in this satire with laughter since Seneca sought to avenge himself, through derision, on the man who had unjustly exiled him. But Seneca was also making another point: emperors were mortals and merited no deification. The ridiculous image of Claudius in Olympus is an exaggerated depiction of any emperor who yearned for immortality. Death, the joyous reaper, has been defeated by Claudius's comical appearance before Hercules; it has been denied the seriousness of the high genres and of the state's religion. The use of vulgar constructions and scatological terms sets the tone for the familiar exchange that supplants the terror associated with death, though the primary objective appears to be Claudius's degradation. Menippus too, if Lucian's *Menippean Satires* accurately mirror his lost works, instead of using the underworld and Olympus for serious philosophical discussions in the manner of his predecessors, mocked these mythical regions and satirized his deceased adversaries.

The Menippea did not lose its impact in the chaotic centuries that followed the fall of Rome. Its dialogical element influenced early Christian literature. In the Christian genres, as in the Menippea, individuals from all walks of life—rulers, rich men, thieves, beggars—meet on an equal, fundamentally dialogized plane. Dream visions, insanity and various types of obsessions enjoy a certain significance here as in the Menippea.

It is not maintained that ancient Christian literature was entirely dependent on the carnivalized Menippea for its structure. Christianity, like the pagan religions it was replacing, entailed ritual festivities and ceremonies as wellsprings for the direct carnivalization of its narrative. Nowhere is this carnivalization more prevalent than in apocryphal Christian literature, which was to prove so instrumental in the formation of European literary genres. Thus, elements of the Menippea and carnivalization—the former a product of the latter—came to exert an undeniable impact on the formation of ancient Christian literature.

In the Middle Ages, Latin ecclesiastical literature, a continuation of the ancient Christian literary tradition, afforded further life to the Menippea. The characteristics of the Menippea can be easily seen in such dialogized and consequently carnivalized medieval genres: "arguments," "debates," ambivalent "panegyrics," morality and miracle plays, and in the later Middle Ages in mystery plays (Gil Vicente's *autos religiosos*) and stories. Secular literature of this period was also saturated with Menippean characteristics: the parodies (*Libro de buen amor*), semiparodies, and especially novelistic literature such as the picaresque.

If, as Bakhtin claims, all medieval theater was carnivalesque, and the entire medieval development of the Menippea was permeated with local carnival folklore, can not Gil Vicente's plays be analyzed using generic characteristics of the Menippea? It should be kept in mind that Portugal had no documented drama prior to Master Gil, a fact that places the founding of Lusitanian drama at almost the onset of the Renaissance, a period of profound carnivalization of literature. With the renewed interest in classical literature wrought by humanism, the Menippea took firm roots in all the major genres.

The brief overview of the carnivalization of literature in this section should not be taken as exhaustive. Our aim was to offer a basic understanding of the tradition and how it persisted through the ages by adaptation and renovation. Our concern is not with the influence exerted by any particular writer, work, theme, idea, or image but with the influence of the serio-comic tradition on our dramatist. Because the Menippea had a far-reaching effect on many genres (major and minor) during the Middle Ages and Renaissance, we shall, in the following chapter, exemplify its characteristics in the plays of Gil Vicente.

3

The Basic Characteristics of the Menippean Satire and Their Application to Vicentine Comedy

In his study on Dostoevsky, Bakhtin lists fourteen characteristics as basic to the ancient Menippea. The purpose of this chapter is to clarify the relationship between this genre and the plays of Gil Vicente by exemplifying each characteristic as found in the Portuguese playwright's works. At times, slight alterations must be made in the definitions of certain characteristics since the Menippea, a most flexible genre, continued its evolution in its postantiquity phase and through the time of Gil Vicente (the waning of the Middle Ages).

Analysis of the Menippean genre in Vicentine comedy exposes the elements of carnivalization in many of the plays, as expected in the Menippea, a thoroughly carnivalized genre. However, carnivalization in Gil Vicente's plays cannot be attributed solely to the Menippea; it has another important direct source: the medieval carnival, a direct descendant of the ancient seasonal festivals such as the Saturnalia. In Master Gil the Menippea (carnival tradition) takes on its proper meaning, which the author combines with other artistic elements to further his aesthetic goals, which in turn vary in accordance with the occasion and its demands for the type of playlet to be composed. We shall see that in even the most serious and nonsatirical plays, Menippean characteristics are incorporated into the structure.

The Menippea displays a variance of the comic element.

The comic element in the Menippea oscillates between a strongly pervasive and a muted presence, which in certain cases all but disappears: in *Don Quixote* for example, the comical aspect is very strong in the first book comparatively and reduced in the second:

73

The phenomenon of reduced laughter is of considerable importance in world literature. Reduced laughter is denied direct expression, which is to say "it does not ring out," but traces of it remain in the structure of the image or a discourse and can be detected in it. Paraphrasing Gogol, one can speak of "laughter invisible to the world." (*Dostoevsky*, 114, n. 4)

Somewhat in the manner of Cervantes, the comic aspect is evident in the farces and comedies of Gil Vicente (the nature of the pieces requires it) and is reduced to a minimum or altogether excluded in his religious and chivalric plays (in *Auto da Alma*, for example, laughter is nonexistent, leading Sebastião Pestana to state: "O *Auto da Alma* nada tem de farsa: não visa a gargalhada balofa e alvar ou até o riso escarninho e amargo").[1] There are certain plays, however, in which one finds a mixture of high and low laughter, as in *Auto da Lusitânia*: the comic element is strong in the first half but greatly reduced in the second.

Among the numerous dramatic and rhetorical devices employed by Master Gil to obtain the desired degrees of laughter are satire (social), parody, sexual and scatological references, puns, visual comedy, comical personal traits, comedy of plot or action, marked contrasts, linguistic peculiarities (speech patterns of certain ethnic and social groups) and clever use of language for comic effect (bathos), proverbs, enumeration of parts of a mangled body ("carnival anatomy"), simple enumeration, and repetition.

In the so-called moralities and mysteries (the religious plays), the comic aspect, when present, had to be significantly mitigated to maintain the religious, somber tone necessary to the plays' didactic aim. Yet, because Gil Vicente's roots were essentially popular, he often resorted to comical techniques in compositions of this type. According to Bakhtin, in many cases laughter continues to determine the structure of the image, but is muted to a minimum: it is as if we hear laughter's footfall but not the laughter itself.

Low-keyed laughter manifests itself in various ways in Vicente's religious plays. In *Auto da História de Deus*, Belial, a devil, angry and jealous because Lucifer has commissioned Satan and not him to tempt Eve and cause her and Adam's fall from grace, concludes the complaint directed at Lucifer by saying:

> Se lá me mandaras, me houvera por cão,
> se não os fizera per força pecar:
> logo per força os fizera tragar
> quantas maçãs naquela árvore estão,
> sem as mastigar.

(2:176)

The mental picture of Adam and Eve being forced to swallow whole one apple after another without even chewing them, and the possible conversion of the devil into a dog if he failed in his task, must have produced a chuckle from the audience.

Toward the conclusion of the play, the three devils gather to discuss Christ's presence on earth and the action they are to take to diminish his impact:

> *Luc.* Digo que este homem nacido em Belém
> parece perigosa cousa pera nós.
> *Bel.* Senhor Lúcifer, isso vede vós,
> porque todo o mal é de quem o tem.
> *Sat.* Dá ó demo a cantiga
> crede que temos com ele fadiga
> que passa de santo.
>
> (2:209-10)

The unexpected appearance of a common expression, a proverb, relaxes the seriousness of the mystery and paves the way for Satan's witty curse ("Dá ó demo a cantiga"). Coming from the mouth of a devil, it must have produced, if not loud laughter, at least some comic relief.

"Carnival anatomy," which in the Menippea and other carnivalized genres was widely used for the purpose of discrowning (a carnival rite to which we shall later return), is adroitly parodied in this play when, after Christ has enumerated the different parts of his body that he will submit to the cruelty of his tormentors, Belial announces his sudden illness and, in popular manner, describes his afflicted bodily parts:

> Senhor Lúcifer, eu ando doente,
> treme-me a cara, e a barba também,
> e dói-me a cabeça, que tal febre tem,
> que soma sam hetigo ordenadamente,
> e dóem-me as canelas:
> sai-me quentura per antre as arnelas,
> e segundo me acho, muito mal me sinto;
> e algum gran desastre me pinta o destinto.
> Até as minhas unhas estão amarelas,
> que é gran labirinto.
>
> (2:214-15)

Also reduced is the comic element found in *Auto da Cananeia*. As in the previous play, the slight hints of laughter are found in the devil's lines. Having been asked by Beelzebub to describe how he had been defeated in his attempt to tempt Christ, Satan responds:

> Eu fiz-me pobre barbato;
> mas é tão gran sabedor,
> que me conheceu milhor
> que eu conheço o meu çapato;
> e ainda que feito pato
> eu lá fora,
> nem convertido, em mulato,
> como o rato sente o gato,
> me sentira logo ess'hora.
>
> (2:242-43)

Here, the images evoked by the distraught devil belong to the marketplace, to the town fair, to the carnival square of the late Middle Ages and Renaissance. Such billingsgate rescues the play from dogmatic seriousness and precludes the possibility of any one point of view becoming absolutized. The devil, though portrayed as the representative of evil, does not appear awesome or supernatural to the reader or audience, but as a scoundrel who, having failed in his objective, attempts a justification.

Further on, his designs once again in jeopardy by the interference of the Apostles, Belial reproaches them with cynical comicalness:

> Oh quem vos mete, senhores,
> em rogardes por ninguém?
> Que, quando rogardes bem
> por vós outros, pecadores,
> ficareis ainda aquém.
> Que vos vai ou que vos vem,
> pois, dabenício,
> assombrar é meu ofício
> e taxados quais e quem?
>
> (2:252-53)

This type of comical reaction vis-à-vis the serious logic of Christ and the Apostles was most common in an era when men were suspicious of seriousness and accustomed to relate sincere and free truth to laughter. Only by the nonofficial element of laughter could Gil Vicente approach the audience, both lords and commoners alike, and produce a mystery in which the human element is so prevalent. As mentioned, the *Auto da Alma* is generally exempt from laughter, for in this allegory the human factor is minimal. Only when the Soul, yielding to the temptation of the Devil, dresses in the manner of a hetaera, are the footprints of laughter discerned in the description.

Laughter resounds louder in *Diálogo sobre a Ressureição*, which contains more comical devices than most of Gil Vicente's religious plays. The initial dialogue between Rabi Levi and Rabi Samuel is laden with proverbs (carnival language) which, along with their peculiar manner of speech, creates the desired comical effect. The comicalness progressively increases by means of repetition ("ha de ser um sonho, que viu um espanto / uã adivinhação, um conto, um chanto, / uã patranha."), satire (the Jews' preoccupation with money: "sonhou que perdia na sisa do trigo"), debasing speech ("andaste às punhadas com algúm rascão, / e quebroi-te os dentes, porque és vilão, / e cuidas que o outro é resucitado"), irony ("pois eram quarenta com armas armados / não no podiam prender oitra vez? / Que razão essa de siso de pez!") and ludicrous genealogical enumeration:

> Meu pai era dono d'ũ filha minha,
> e minha mãe filha do meu dono torto
> e um meu irmão, que morreu no Porto.
> era mesmo tio dos filhos qu'eu tinha:
> tudo assi vai.
> E minha mulher, nora de meu pai;
> e meu pai, marido de sua mulher;
> e a sua mulher era sogra da minha.
> Assi indo fomos, de linha em linha,
> até que meu pai veio a morrer.
> Meu pai falecido,
> vai minha mãe e perdeu o marido,
> e fez-se viúva, e as alcaçarias
> foram do pai da mãe de Tobias,
> filha de Dom Donegal dolorido,
> que morreu nas Pias.
> E quando se fez a tomada de Arzila,
> Dona Franca Pomba casou em Buarcos
> Com Bento Capaio, capador dos gatos,
> que furando alporcas, morreu em Tavila.
>   Em aqueles dias
> se fez o contrato das alcaçarias,
> e David Ladainhas da manga cagada
> leixou assentado, que vindo o Messias
> que as alcaçarias, não tendo elas nada,
> que fossem vasias.
>
>   (2:228-29)

References to the lower bodily parts—*manga cagada* (excrement) and *capador de gatos*—increase the resonance of the laughter already elicited by the farcical description of lineage. Such references have an additional structural design: to counterbalance Christ's resurrection and ascension (upward directed) by focusing the spectators' attention downward on the lower strata of the body. This is a common carnival device found in the Menippea.

Amadis de Gaula, a satirical work, parodies the epic hero of the chivalric novel from which it derives its title. As T. P. Waldron so aptly puts it:

> In *Amadis de Gaula* the salient features are irony and burlesque, and the result is a tenuous balance between a serious plot, developed with considerable dramatic insight, and an undercurrent of raillery which at any moment is liable to destroy the pretence.[2]

Instead of creating a pathetic atmosphere, since the play does not deal with the trials and tribulations of a lovesick knight, Master Gil repeatedly brings about bathetic situations that maintain the plot on its semicomic course. Warned by the Messenger that seven kings with large armies are advancing to make war on his kingdom, King Lisuarte points out:

> No está en la mucha gente
> la victoria de razon,
> sino en la devocion,
> y resar continuamente,
> las horas de la pasion.

To which the Messenger responds:

> Señor, no os atengais á eso;
> sabed que en fin de razones
> para el perro que es travieso
> bueno palo, valiente y grueso,
> y no cureis de oraciones.
>
> (4:13)

The marked contrast between the monarch's deeply religious, lofty thought and the messenger's earthly, wise observation demolishes any romantic overtones in the play.

Likewise, a situation of attenuated humor arises when Amadis, doing penance for his unrequited love, returns to the hermitage accompanied by the hermit with whom he has been seeking alms:

> Erm.   La limosna sea cerrada,
> porque hay dos mil ratones
> en esta ermita cuitada.
> Ama.   Yo la porné tan guardada

como guardo mis pasiones.
Erm. Y con esta escoba, hermano,
barrereis esta posada.—
Porque alzais ansí la mano?
Ama. Perdonad, padre ermitano,
que yo pensé que era espada.

(4:50-51)

The sharp contrasts in this dialogue—mice/passions, broom /sword—are amusing oxymoronic combinations typical of *mésalliances*; in this case, the *mesálliance* brought about by a self-willed discrowning, i.e., the surrender by Amadis of his knightly attire and donning of hermitic garb. However, as in carnival, such discrowning bears within it the seeds of coronation: Amadis, upon reading the letter sent by Oriana, decides to forgo his life of contrition and returns to his former self.

Naturally, in the farces and comedies laughter knows no restraints. This is not to imply that the sole purpose of these works was to entertain and produce humorous situations because, alongside the drollery, a constant preoccupation of Gil Vicente was the desire to deliver a moral message. The rapid deterioration of morals and ethics in the Portugal of his time appears to have affected him profoundly. As an artist, he believed strongly that *risus castigat mores*, a fact to which his farces and comedies bear witness.

Such a desire to alter customs by reprehending with laughter, led Gil Vicente, like Aristophanes in antiquity, to compose plays best described as a blend of the serious and the comic. Aubrey F. G. Bell corroborates this observation:

He [Gil Vicente] defied every rule of Aristotle and mingled together the grave and gay, the coarse and courtly in a way faithful to life rather than to any accepted theories of the stage.[3]

In *Farsa de Inês Pereira*, sexuality is exploited to maximum humoristic effect when Lianor Vaz, recounting her frightening encounter with a cleric, explains his designs: "Diz que havia de saber / se era eu fêmea se macho" (5:224). That the cleric used such ruse to seduce Lianor is in itself funny, but what renders the episode even more comic are the terms employed by the cleric—*fêmea* and *macho*—nouns differentiating animal genders and not *homem* and *mulher*, as would befit human beings.

Taken aback by the cleric's temerity, Lianor asks, "Jesu! homem que hás contigo?" He responds, "Irmã, eu t'assolverei co breviário de Braga" (5:224). Carolina Michaëlis de Vasconcelos confesses, in respect to this breviary, that she was unable to come to any conclusion about its definite meaning.[4] Mention of such a breviary in the piece appears to be a play on words with the proper noun *Braga* which, though a direct reference to the Portuguese city, is also a type of pants formerly worn by men.[5] Since the anecdote is a narrative of attempted rape, the vestiary meaning is logical and would have certainly elicited guffaws from the audience—two other possible wordplays are: *breviário* (breviary) with *breve* (short), in reference to his reproductive organ; and *braga* with *braguilha* (fly of men's trousers). After concluding her account, Lianor is asked by Inês's mother, "Mana, conhecia-t'ele?" to which she answers, "Mas' queria-me conhecer." Once again, sexual connotation underscores the comicalness of the farce.

Scatological references are also utilized by Master Gil to enhance comicalness. In the same play, after introducing themselves, Latam and Vidal, the two Jewish matchmakers, begin to complain of how far they had to travel and the many inconveniences suffered in order to find Inês a mate. Latam swears that, "assi me fadem boas fadas / que me saltou caganeira" (5:239). Punning with lower bodily functions is another comedy-sustaining device; for instance, in *Triunfo do Inverno* the cabin boy does not understand an order from the pilot and gives the ensuing comical etymology of the nautical term *traquete* (foresail):

> E quem he aqui o traquete?
> O traque sei eu que he,
> mas o quete não sei eu
> inda agora onde elle s'he.
>
> (4:292)

Visual or physical comicalness is frequent in the more humorous plays. In one example Pero Marques, in *Farsa de Inês Pereira*, sits with his back to Inês, for he had never sat on a chair and did not know how to sit properly. In *Floresta de Enganos* a philandering doctor, by a girl's deceit, is forced to impersonate a woman and to sift flour.

Another recourse is the depiction of comical personal traits. For instance, Pero Marques's shyness leads to his reluctance to remain in the dark alone with Inês. The different temperaments of the four brothers in *Farsa do Juiz da Beira* motivate many hilarious episodes: the lout, who only sleeps and snores; the dancer, who wants only to dance; the lover, who is constantly complaining about the ills of love; and the swordsman, who speaks solely of deeds of bravery though he is himself a coward. The four squabble over an ass bequeathed them by their deceased father.

Comicalness of plot or action also sustains a high degree of laughter throughout certain pieces, such as the serenading of Isabel by the squire in *Quem Tem Farelos?* or the imbroglio arising in *Auto da Índia* from the husband's absence. Among numerous examples of hilarity that permeate these two works, this excerpt from a dialogue between Ordoño and Apariço in *Quem Tem Farelos?* illustrates the jocose intention of the poet:

> *Apa.* Está na pele,
> que lhe fura já a ossada
> não comemos quase nada
> eu e o cavalo, nem ele.
> E se o visses brasonar,
> e fingir mais d'esforçado;
> e todo o dia aturado
> se lhe vai em se gabar
>   Estoutro dia, ali num beco,
> deram-lhe tantas pancadas,
> tanta, tantas, que aosadas!...
> *Ord.* Y con qué?
> *Apa.* Cum arrocho seco.
> *Ord.* Hi hi hi hi hi hi hi.
> *Apa.* Folguei tanto!
> *Ord.* Y él callar?
> *Apa.* E ele calar e levar,
> assi assi, ma ora, assi!
>
> (5:59-60)

Sebastião Pestana, though not acquainted with Bakhtin's literary theories, was well aware of Master Gil's intent:

Tudo aqui se acumula para a explosão e alimento do uso sincero, espontâneo e continuado: desde a oposição, que é, no trecho, a sua parede mestra—valentia-pusilanimidade—até as circunstâncias, a que não falta sequer a de "lugar" de suma valia, a citação indefinida da pancadaria de moiro, o consolo sem par que a interjeição traduz, e nisso vai de mãos dadas com ela o corte cerce do fio do pensamento, que, de consecutivo, inicialmente, entra, e lá se queda, no círculo da exclamação, o instrumento do castigo e o sítio, verdadeiramente decepcionante, impeditivo duma fuga a tempo, a gargalhada do espanhol, sinceramente colaborante, a imitação expressiva das vergastadas—tudo se harmoniza para manter tensa a dupla finalidade em vista: sátira social, e de tal modo contundente, que o fidalgo, ele mesmo, sai dela desfeiteado e a sangrar, ironia mordaz, subtil e graciosa, largamente alimentadora da risada natural e escarninha.[6]

The oxymoronic combination bravery/pusillanimity, common to carnival, along with the inherent social satire, will be examined later in this chapter.

As previously observed, Gil Vicente relied heavily on the linguistic peculiarities of given ethnic and social groups for his humorous effect: the macaronic Latin of doctors and judges (*Auto dos Físicos* and *Barca do Inferno*); the popular speech—*sayagués*—of rustics (*Auto Pastoril Castelhano* and *Auto dos Reis Magos*); and the Portuguese of Negroes (*Frágoa de Amor*), gypsies (*Farsa das Ciganas*), Moors (*Cortes de Júpiter*), and Frenchmen and Italians (*Auto da Fama*).

It was mentioned earlier that Master Gil used ploys to avert pathos, which would seriously undermine his parodic designs. In *Amadis de Gaula*, we saw that bathos was achieved by sharp contrast in the language used by two characters. Another example of such clever use of language for comic effect is found in *Comédia de Rubena*: Felício, bemoaning in the mountains his misfortunes in love, is answered by the surrounding range (echo):

> *Fel.* Que será, o quem, ou donde,
> que ande em valle tão sêco?
> *Eco.* Eco.
> . . . .
> *Fel.* Ando qual nunca foi tal
> Ó voz, pois que me respondes,
> e de mi assi t'escondes,
> que farei a tanto mal?
> *Eco.* Al.

(3:73-74)

The Menippea is totally free from historical limitations and evinces an extraordinary freedom of philosophical and creative invention.

The Menippea is fully liberated from the limitations of the historical forms characteristic of such carnivalized genres as the Socratic dialogue. Unrestricted by any requirement of external verisimilitude, it is characterized by an unususal degree of philosophical latitude and of creativity within the plot. Bakhtin observes that:

The fact that the leading heroes of the menippea are historical and legendary figures (Diogenes, Menippus and others) presents no obstacle. Indeed, in all of world literature we could not find a genre more free than the menippea in its invention and use of the fantastic. (*Dostoevsky*, 114)

Such is the case in *Auto da Lusitânia*, in which Gil Vicente gives free rein to his imaginative powers and creates a fantastic nationalistic allegory not without its moments of masterful realistic depiction. After including a view of a typical day in a Jewish household, the play suddenly veers to an illusory recounting of Portugal's origins. A licentiate, appearing out of nowhere, reveals that a sibyl divulged the biographical secrets of ancient Portugal to Gil Vicente, our poet. Such an unexpected change of events creates a kind of play within a play that exemplifies the liberties taken in the composition of the piece. Later, in the same play, this fantastic depiction of national origins is followed by an even more improbable association, more lacking in verisimilitude than the allegory itself: two devils, Dinato and Berzebu, serve as chaplains to the pagan goddesses. Notice the incongruities in the dialogue between the two devils:

> *Din.* No saber universal
> crê que meu spirito voa.
> *Ber.* Queres uma cousa boa?
> Antes que entremos ao al
> rezemos a sexta e noa,
> e depois todalas horas
> das negligências mundanas,
> em louvor das soberanas
> diesas nossas senhoras
> e milagrosas Troianas.
> *Din.* Ora rezemos parceiro,
> e porque seja melhor,
> toma, vês hi o salteiro
> de Nabucodonosor,
> que lhe furtou Frei Sueiro.
> *Ber.* Quem começará primeiro?
> *Din.* Tu que és amancebado,
> e és padre verdadeiro,
> que tens filhos ao teu lado,
> e eu sam ainda solteiro.

(6:79-80)

Not only are the devils about to pray to the pagan goddesses, fanciful enough in itself, but the reference to a Psalter of Nebuchadnezzar is simply preposterous. The dialogue seems to reflect Master

Gil's ambivalence toward the Renaissance modes then beginning to dictate artistic creations; while realizing that it was fashionable to incorporate mythological beings into a work, at the same time he had no wish to omit entirely the religious (biblical/Christian) elements so typical of medieval representations. His dislike for pagan deities is here manifested by the alliance of the forces of evil with such entities. He also uses the opportunity to chide clerics who ignore their vows of celibacy.

In *Frágoa de Amor*, a play based entirely on fantastical elements, a Negro enters the forge and exits converted into a white man, as was his desire; however, his speech remains that of a black man. Dismayed, he laments his fate; henceforth, he will please neither white nor black women, for he now belongs to neither race. This seems to mirror the author's belief that a person should be content with his or her lot in life.

After the Negro, Justice appears, in the form of a hunchbacked old woman. She desires to be rejuvenated and straightened, but the initial attempt is unsuccessful. Jupiter then remarks to Cupid:

> Señor, nuestro martillar
> no nos aprovecha nada,
> porque la Justicia dañada,
> los que mas la han de emendar
> la hacen mas corcovada.
>
> (4:118)

Such an observation is an attack on the corrupt legal system of the era. After another attempt, the forgers (the Planets) succeed in giving Justice her desired appearance. Then, a friar without any vocation appears asking to be transformed into a layman. He lists the desired traits and, as examples, names men well known to the audience. Cupid replies that he will do as the friar asks only if permission is granted by the friar's abbot. The friar then leaves to seek permission and, in the interim, two squires and a fool arrive to convey their masters' desires. These masters are, once again, real-life individuals well known to all those present at the performance. It is not made clear what changes the master of the first squire desires, but Cupid, finding him flawless, refuses to make any alterations. The friar returns after obtaining permission and asks to be transformed into a soldier. Cupid grants him his wish and the play comes to an end.

In his dialogue with the first squire, Cupid abandons chronological sequence in describing the perfection of the master:

Y pues lo hizo Anibal,
caballero tan famoso,
si yo refundir lo oso,
como se hará otro tal?

(4:123)

This freedom from historical limitations is quite common in the plays of Gil Vicente and in no way detracts from the plot; what seemingly destroys external verisimilitude adds to the fantastic dénouement by imparting an air of grandeur. A case in point is *Auto da Sibila Cassandra*, where prophets of the Old Testament meet with the Sibyls of ancient Greece and Rome to prophesy the birth and passion of Christ. In *Triunfo do Inverno*, the Sintra mountain range, personified, suggests to Spring a fine gift for the Portuguese princess Dona Isabel, on her birthday: Sintra's beautiful gardens, which:

que Salamão mandou aqui
a hum Rei de Portugal;
e tem-no seu filho ali.

(4:326)

Though the anachronism is here intentional, there are occasions on which the author's forgetfulness or carelessness seems to produce lapses of chronology as in *Floresta de Enganos* when the philosopher, chained by the leg to a fool, opens the play by saying:

Asegun siento mis males,
al discreto singular
gran pena le es conversar
con los necios perenales,
sin lo poder escusar.
Los muy antiguos Romanos,
comenzando á ser tiranos,
porque Roma se ofendia,
yo por mi filosofía,
les di consejos muy sanos.

(3:169)

According to Carolina Michaëlis de Vasconcelos, "confundindo épocas, o poeta pensava por ventura em Séneca."[7]

Also common are the unannounced lapses of time and sudden changes of setting without explanation. The departure of Constança's husband in *Auto da Índia* and her ensuing infidelities appear to take place from one day to the next. Finding herself alone after having sent away her Spanish suitor, Constança is approached by her maid; their exchange runs as follows:

> *Moç.* Ando dizendo entre mi,
> que agora vai em dous anos
> que eu fui lavar os panos
> além do chão d'Alcami;
> e logo partiu a armada
> domingo de madrugada.
> Não pode muito tardar
> nova se há-de tornar
> noss'amo pera a pousada.
>
> *Ama.* Asinha.
> *Moç.*   Tres anos há
> que partiu Tristão da Cunha.
> *Ama.* Cant'eu ano e meio punha.
> *Moç.* Mas três e mais haverá.

                                                    (5:108)

The audience is completely taken aback by the length of time that has passed; furthermore, distinct discrepancies are evident: whereas the maid stated that the fleet departed at dawn on a Sunday two years before, now she says it was three years; finally, after her mistress mentions that the elapsed time was one and a half years, she corrects both mistress and herself, giving three and a half years as the period.

One may argue that the discrepancy is intentional and that it represents a dramatic foreshortening of a whole series of similar adventures with which the *ama* has amused herself during her husband's absence. This argument is not, however, convincing; it is more likely that Vicente was unaware of inconsistencies in his text, or confident that his audience would not notice them.[8]

Whether the playwright was aware of the existing discrepancies, as Thomas R. Hart argues above, is in itself irrelevant; the extraordinary freedom of invention afforded by the Menippea allowed him to focus his attention primarily on his twin creative concerns of entertainment and satire. Had Gil Vicente adhered to the Aristotelian dramatic unities of time, space, and action, his theatrical compositions would have been greatly restricted and in all likelihood far less interesting.

Another play with similar inconsistencies is *Farsa do Velho da Horta*. Here Master Gil seems oblivious to external verisimilitude, as several examples illustrate. No mention is made, for example, of how or when the Girl left the orchard after the Old Man's gallantries; if it was indeed night when the Fool entered the orchard, as his question to the Old Man suggests—"que fazeis vós cá té à noute?" (5:152)—when did the subsequent scenes take place? How did the Fool fetch the guitar requested by the Old Man and return without a noticeable interruption in the conversation of the two men? Free invention characterizes the final stages of the piece; the scenes involving the panderess, her arrest by law officers, and the arrival of the young girl (a buyer) who announces to the Old Man that his Dulcinea has just married a young man, take place with total disregard for verisimilitude. The scenes have no nexus, leaving the impression that the wedding was hurriedly held at night.

The inclusion of well-known personalities and of legendary figures in the plays was a common device used by the poet to add gravity or, more frequently, humor—as in *Frágoa de Amor*—and such inclusion enhanced rather than restricted creative freedom. In *Farsa do Velho da Horta*, the panderess's litany invokes contemporary courtiers (who have been canonized as martyrs of love) to come to the aid of the unconscious Old Man. In the words of Segismundo Spina:

A ladainha onomástica da Alcoviteira, apelando para as virtudes sortílegas daquela galeria de santos prematuros, se hoje não faria sentido na representação da farsa, devia corresponder ao momento culminante no cómico pela atualidade da cena: as figuras invocadas eram pessoas da corte e os próprios espectadores.[9]

Such was the freedom of invention exhibited by Gil Vicente that he did not hesitate to have his name mentioned by the characters or to even include himself in several of the plays. An example of the former is *Auto dos Físicos*, in which a fictitious lovesick priest is visited by four medical doctors who attempt to diagnose his illness. The physicians espouse all the medical theories then popular but fail to pinpoint the real nature of the priest's illness, i.e., a broken heart. A priest-confessor is summoned and confesses that he, too, has been love-stricken for many a year. He then absolves the patient because God has ordained that no one should be punished for being in love. The priest-confessor prepares to leave and divulges his destination and purpose:

Voyme á la huerta de amores
y traeré una ensalada
por Gil Vicente guisada,
y diz que otra de mas flores

para Pascua tien sembrada.

(6:127)

The *ensalada* to which he refers was a poetic medley of verses from other popular poems. By including himself indirectly in the text, Gil Vicente both propagandized himself as a poet and anticipated another medley of this sort that he hoped to introduce at Easter.

In *Templo de Apolo*, Master Gil appears in person at the beginning of the piece to excuse himself for what he felt was an imperfect play. He blames its inferiority on the illness he suffered during its composition and rambles on about an extravagant dream he had had while ill, to underscore his delirious state.

Though the Menippea is fully liberated from the limitations of the memoir form common to Socratic dialogue, the form is sometimes preserved externally; Master Gil's exculpation at the outset is an excellent example of the rare external use of the memoir form in a Menippea-related genre.

Gil Vicente was well aware of the complete freedom of invention that he enjoyed. Nowhere is this more apparent than in *Auto da Mofina Mendes*, in which a friar delivers a burlesque sermon laden with dialectical verbiage warning the audience about the play it is about to see:

> He de notar,
> que haveis de considerar
> isto ser contemplação
> fora da história geral,
> mas fundada em devação.
> . . . .
> Será logo o fundamento
> trata da saudação.
> e depos deste sermão,
> hum pouco do nacimento;
> tudo por nova invenção.

(1:132)

In the Menippea, the wildest fantastic situations are brought into organic and indissoluble artistic unity with the philosophical idea to provoke and test the truth.

One of the most important characteristics of the Menippea is the justification and illumination of the most unrestricted fantasies and adventures by an essential ideological and philosophical purpose.

The creation of unusual situations, internally induced, gives rise to and examines the philosophical idea of the truth. The fantastic, it should be emphasized, does not serve as the absolute incarnation of the truth. Rather, it searches for the truth, both provoking and testing it. Bakhtin goes on to say that:

> To this end the heroes of the "Menippean satire" ascend into heaven, descend into the nether world, wander through unknown and fantastic lands, are placed in extraordinary life situations (Diogenes, for example, sells himself into slavery in the marketplace, Peregrinus triumphantly immolates himself at the Olympic Games, Lucius the Ass finds himself constantly in extraordinary situations). Very often the fantastic takes on the character of an adventure story; sometimes it assumes a symbolic or even mystical-religious character (as in Apuleius). But in all of these instances the fantastic is subordinated to the purely ideational function of provoking and testing the truth. The most unrestrained and fantastic adventures are present here in organic and indissoluble artistic unity with the philosophical idea. And it is essential to emphasize once again that the issue is precisely the testing of an *idea*, of a *truth*, and not the testing of a particular human character, whether an individual or a social type. The testing of a wise man is a test of his philosophical position in the world, not a test of any other features of his character independent of that position. In this sense one can say that the content of the menippea is the adventures of an *idea* or a *truth* in the world: either on earth, in the nether regions, or on Olympus. (*Dostoevsky*, 114-15)

The purpose of medieval religious plays was to bring forth and exemplify Christian ideas or truths and, in this sense, such plays were merely a modified medieval dramatic rendition of the Menippea. However, these ideas or truths were not elevated to the level of the absolute by realistic or logical presentations. A true-to-life presentation would only have rendered the production sterile, given its inability to illustrate a concept that relied so heavily on the audience's faith and imagination. Extraordinary situations were therefore created, freed from all conditions, positions, obligations, and laws of normal life.

In *Auto Pastoril Castelhano*, Gil Vicente's first religious play, a mystery, the explanation of Christ's miraculous birth (held as an absolute Christian truth) falls to a shepherd, Gil Terron, whose rustic background would seem to contradict his demonstrated erudition.

As with Menippean heroes, the fact that Gil Terron is possessed by the "truth" determines his attitude toward others and creates his special kind of loneliness:

> *Bras.* [a shepherd]   Dí, Gil Terron, tú qué has,

Gil.
que siempre andas apartado?
. . . .
repastando mis cabritas
por estas sierras benditas:
no me acuerdo del lugar.
Cuando, cara al cielo, oteo,
y veo tan buena cosa,
no me parece hermosa
ni de asseo
zagala de cuantas veo.

Andando solo magino,
que la soldada que gano
se me pierde de la mano
soncas en qualquier camino.
Nesta soledad me enseño;
que el ganado com que ando,
no sabré como ni cuando,
segun sueño,
quizá será de otro dueño.

(1:11-12)

Unlike in most Menippeas, where persons knowing the truth are ridiculed as madmen by others, here Gil Terron is merely solicited to be more gregarious and, when he declines, his preference for solitude is respected. This conversation also prefigures the uncommon knowledge Gil Terron exhibits at the Nativity manger when quizzed by his peers.

After receiving word from an angel that Christ has been born, Gil Terron, with fellow shepherds, rushes to the site. He then explains to his fellows doctrines relating to the Virgin, whom he identifies as the wife and shepherdess mentioned by Solomon in his Song of Songs; with respect to Christ, he quotes prophecies of his birth as the Son of God. His entire narration is sprinkled with biblical and liturgical Latin phrases that astound the listening rustics all the more. The play ends with this explicative exchange:

Bra. Gil Terron lletrudo está:
muy hondo te encaramillas!
Gil. Dios hace estas maravillas.
Bra. Ya lo veo, soncas ha.

Quien te viere no dirá,
que naciste en serrania.

(1:31)

This drama displays a fantastic adventure of a mystical-religious character bent on provoking and testing an undisputed truth: that the prophecies about Christ's birth and humble origins were correct. To this end the playwright ignores actual time and place: Christ is (re)born in sixteenth-century Iberia. Because the testing here is that of a Christian truth rather than that of a character's social standing, there is no objection to the presence of a learned country bumpkin; as he himself explains: "God performs these wonders."

Noteworthy is the fact that, in the compositions of Juan del Encina and Lucas Fernández—the Spanish primitives who are said to have influenced heavily Master Gil's early pieces—the birth of the Savior consistently takes place, as it should, in Bethlehem. The Spanish shepherds must set out for this site, and never is the Nativity scene incorporated into the body of any text.

In the mystery *Auto da Sibila Cassandra*, one of Vicente's most unrestricted fantasies, the objective is to awaken Cassandra to the reality that she is not to be the Virgin chosen by God to bear His Son. Thomas R. Hart's 1958 rigid allegorical interpretation of the play in "Gil Vicente's *Auto de la Sibila Casandra*" led, either directly or indirectly, to articles by I. S. Révah, M. R. Lida de Malkiel, and Leo Spitzer dealing primarily with the possible sources of the piece as well as its artistic unity. Observations made in the three studies point to the pitfalls and, at times, contradictions inherent in Hart's approach to this play.[10]

At the beginning of the play she rejects the shepherd Salomão's marriage proposal on the grounds that marriage is a type of slavery and opts for spinsterhood. Salomão summons her aunts (the Sibyls): Erutea, Peresica, and Ciméria. These in turn summon the girl's uncles (the Prophets): Esaias, Moyses, and Abrahão. At this point, Cassandra reveals her premonition and her uncles chide her for her presumptuousness; along with the aunts, they cite scriptural and apocryphal prophecies to dissuade the credulous girl. Then curtains open to reveal the Nativity scene and angels singing. All praise the Virgin and Child! Cassandra, realizing her mistake, declares:

> Señor, yo, de ya perdida
> nesta vida,
> no te oso pedir nada,
> porque nunca di pasada
> concertada;
> ni debiera ser nacida.
> Vírgen y madre de Dios,
> á vos, á vos,
> corona de las mugeres,

por vuestros siete placeres,
que quieras rogar por nos.

(1:79)

The idea or truth tested in this play is that presumptuousness is a human fault that runs counter to the humility demanded by Christian doctrine. The characters, therefore, are mere symbols used for the evocation and testing of the idea: Cassandra, human presumptuousness; the Virgin, humility glorified; the aunts and uncles, sibyls and prophets who foretell events well known to the audience. This disparate group of characters and the sudden unexpected appearance of the Nativity scene present an extraordinary setting geared to represent Christ's coming and his tragic fate, and to eliminate Cassandra's haughty pretensions. Her recognition and repentance of the wrong committed by her symbolize the inevitable victory of humility over presumptuousness, for she truly humbled herself by rejecting her former false notions.

Another daring and unfettered fantasy is *Auto da Feira*, in which our dramatist's Erasmian philosophy creates a fair where the forces of good and evil set up shop to sell their wares to whoever will buy them, the Church included. With regard to this play, António J. Saraiva and Óscar Lopes observe:

Gil Vicente participa no grande debate de *idéias* que agita a primeira metade do século XVI e que assume principalmente a forma de discussões teológicas. Alguns do seus autos, e especialmente o *Auto da Feira*, intervêm na polémica religiosa. Circumstâncias peculiares, entre as quais os litígios de D. João III com o clero nacional e com a Santa Fé, e as violentas dissenções entre o Papa e Carlos V, cunhado do rei de Portugal, que culminaram no saque e incêndio de Roma em 1527, deram-lhe oportunidade para, neste campo, ir muito mais longe do que qualquer outro autor português do século XVI.[11]

Mercury, after a brief introduction attacking astrologers and superstition, announces a fair and, immediately, Time enters setting up a tent with many things long forgotten by humanity: virtues, counsel, justice, truth, and peace. At his request, a seraph appears who summons the Church to attend:

Á feira, á feira, igrejas, mosteiros,
pastores das almas, Papas adormidos;
comprae aqui panos, mudae os vestidos,
buscae as çamarras dos outros primeiros
os antecessores.

(1:205)

The Devil, likewise, sets up a small tent as though he were a vendor of trinkets. His wares are deceits, ambition, wickedness, hypocrisy, and imprudence. The first customer is Rome, who enters singing and who desires to buy peace, truth, and faith. The Devil tempts her. She does not allow herself to be seduced and complains of having endured some rough times for previously having bought certain things from him, which she fails to specify. Approaching Time's tent, she asks the seraph to sell her "peace in heaven" in exchange for which she will give him jubilees.

Mercury intervenes to criticize Rome and orders Time to give him the coffer of his (Mercury's) counsels. A mirror that belonged to the Virgin is given to Rome, in which she will find the path to righteousness.

Rome departs and the second half begins. Two farmers, Amancio Vaz and Deniz Lourenço, enter. These are discontented with their wives, Branca Annes, the rough one, and Marta Dias, the gentle one. The women make their appearance criticizing their husbands and curse the hour in which they were married. Having overheard their wives' conversation, the farmers decide to leave them and turn their attention to the village girls. Both wives approach the Devil's tent first, then Time's. Instead of the clear conscience that the seraph attempts to sell them, they opt for knickknacks and luxuries.

Nine mountain girls and three youths appear with baskets on their heads. They desire nothing of what the seraph has to sell as their purpose for coming to the fair is to pay homage to the Holy Virgin. The play ends with the girls singing in two choruses a lay to the Virgin.

Many are the symbols in this parable, beginning with the marketplace itself. This marketplace is a microcosm of the world where the individual, because of materialistic inclinations, often bypasses or completely ignores spiritual values. Mercury, Time, and the seraph represent the word of God, the forces of good, while the Devil stands for ephemeral earthly delights and, consequently, all that is evil. Rome is the symbol of the Church gone astray and in need of reform. The farmers' wives, Branca and Marta, typify man's preference for transitory earthly joys over spiritual concerns. The twelve peasants who appear late in the play, though uninterested in the seraph's wares, a fact that seems to link them to all individuals who shun spirituality, have nevertheless a purpose for coming to the marketplace other than the acquisition of material things: to pay homage to the Holy Virgin.

Hence, their indifference to spiritual matters stems not from a considered preference but from sheer ignorance. This demonstrated simplicity is representative of individuals who know not what they do; for them, as for children, the kingdom of Heaven is always accessible. It should be emphasized that the mere fact that these twelve characters were peasants does not bespeak the playwright's intention to test a given social group; what is tested here is the concept that those who act not from malice, but from ignorance, should be forgiven and corrected.

As is customary in the Menippea, Vicente's plays on occasion take on the character of an adventure story through time and space. In *Comédia de Rubena*, a fantastic production in three acts, Rubena, an abbot's daughter, becomes pregnant by a priest. A sorceress brought by a midwife conjures up four little devils that transport Rubena through the air to a mountain where she gives birth to a daughter, Cismena. As António J. Saraiva and Óscar Lopes observe:

> E na primeira cena da *Comédia de Rubena*, a parteira faz entrar no quarto da menina grávida e queixosa um vento poderoso que expulsa todas as pieguices para só deixar lugar à vida, que é mágica e animal, burlesca e grandiosa acima de todas as convenções humanas.[12]

It appears, then, that the midwife serves to introduce the dramatist's philosophical idea: life's supremacy over human conventions.

The second act shifts from Rubena's misfortunes as a lonely mountain girl to Cismena's upbringing by the sorceress. The latter summons four fairies who predict the girl's future; suddenly the scene changes, showing us a five-year-old Cismena who has become a shepherdess and is now weaving. The conversation that ensues between Cismena and three young shepherds, Joane, Pedrinho, and Afonsinho, attests to Gil Vicente's ability to reproduce the speech patterns of the various segments of Portuguese society of his day. Here, we have not only a sample of the language of rustics, but also, for the first time in Portuguese literature, the simplicity of children's speech:

Ped.	Ta mãe não faz senão chamar...
	E tu ris-te, Cismeninha?
Cis.	Rio-me eu da tua tinha.
Ped.	Outra vez t'ha d'ella dar.
Cis.	Toma pera tua vida.
Aff.	Porque davas ontem gritos?
Cis.	Porque comeu dous cabritos
	hũa raposa parida.

Ped. Eu comi papas aquesta.
Aff. E minha mãe deu-me hum bolo.
Joa. Qués-me tu dar delle, tolo?
Cis. Outro levo eu ca na cesta.
Ped. Ja pario a nossa bêsta.
Joa. E nós temos tanto mel,
que trouge a nossa Isabel!
Aff. Mentes, Joane.
Joa. Par esta.

(3:41-42)

The fairies, sensing the time has come for their predictions to come true, encourage Cismena to set out for Crete, where she will be adopted by a wealthy lady whose riches Cismena is to inherit at the age of fifteen.

The third act opens with the prophecy having been fulfilled and Cismena lamenting her unstable life. She is wooed by many suitors. A prince from Syria visits Crete, falls in love with her from afar and, disguised as a page, decides to serve one of her suitors, Felicio, so that he may see her up close. Spurned by Cismena, Felicio, accompanied by the prince, returns to the desert to die of a broken heart. The prince then confronts Cismena with the news and reveals his true identity. He asks for her hand in marriage; she refuses on grounds that her virtue is not for sale. The prince, however, insists and attempts to set her mind at ease:

Mas alta, dice Platon,
es la virtud que el estado;
y a esta es obligado
el mundo de darle el don,
y el cetro mas honrado.

(3:82)

Cismena, convinced that this is indeed *amor verdadeiro*, decides to marry the prince. A chorus of embroideresses concludes the play by exclaiming: "Senhora, não mais costura; / festejemos tal ventura, / ventura bem empregada."

From this conclusion, there should be no doubt that Master Gil's objective was the provocation of a philosophical idea and its testing by the creation of a fantastic adventure. Cismena's illegitimate origins (the daughter and granddaughter of priests), her transportation in her mother's womb to a mountain by devils, her childhood as a shepherdess, and the journey from Spain to Crete, where she meets the Syrian prince, are all unfettered fantasies created to exemplify a philosophical position: virtue triumphs over environmental and hereditary factors and is rewarded by true love. True love in this instance also overcomes social inequality.

The perennial struggle between the forces of Good and Evil, a common medieval motif, is skillfully set in *Auto da Alma* for the purpose of illustrating the *raison d'être* of the Holy Church (the philosophical idea). On its "journey" through this life, the frivolous human soul (Alma) is constantly tempted by the Devil (Diabo) while instructed by a guardian angel (Anjo Custódio) in spiritual matters. St. Augustine affirms at the outset of the piece the need for a *pousada* in which all souls may find repose; such an inn is the Holy Mother Church (*Santa Madre Igreja*). Tired because of the Devil's temptations, the Soul resolves to seek refuge in an inn (the Church) and consequently repents having yielded to vanity, lust, and greed. After a mystical repast served by the Church Fathers (St. Augustine, St. Ambrose, St. Jerome, and St. Thomas), the soul brings the allegory to an end by glorifying the Almighty.

It has been said that before Gil Vicente the medieval dramatic conflict of the soul's vacillation between right and wrong had never been presented within the framework of a journey.[13] In this play, the "journey" concept considerably aids the dialogical syncrisis (the *pro et contra* concerning the religious question at hand). The abrupt change in the Soul's outlook on evil is plausible only if movement through time and space has been understood all along. But inasmuch as the primary objective seems to be the exemplification of the Church's role in Christian life, the "journey" is used symbolically to explain why the soul had wearied and had therefore decided to enter the inn for a rest.

As in the Menippea, Vicentine heroes are sometimes placed in extraordinary situations in order to test their mettle. Such is the case of Pero Marques in *Farsa do Juiz da Beira*, where the boor, husband to Inês Pereira, has been named district judge. Because of his rumored simple-minded, arbitrary judgments, he is asked to set up his *audiência* before the king himself. The common sense he demonstrates in deciding each case reminds one of Sancho Panza on the island of Barataria and may well have inspired Cervantes.

In the different cases and corresponding judgments by Pero Marques, we find the exposition of Gil Vicente's beliefs: many rapes are induced by the violated party and the fact that the panderess's daughter did not scream while being raped underscores the author's view. The panderess, whose profession is considered (by Gil Vicente) an indispensable national institution, is exempt from any wrongdoing in the defilement of the Jew's daughter. The decision in the case of the squire's servant whose boss had not paid him his due wages goes against a class that lived indolently from the profits of the peasant's toil: the squire was obliged to indemnify his servant.

Although in the Vicentine comedies the heroes do not ascend into Heaven or descend into the nether world with the frequency of their counterparts in the Menippea, there is at least one instance in which subordinate characters descend into Hell to bring renowned ancient figures back to earth. These would voice the playwright's opinions on love and the Portuguese nation. Such an instance is found in *Exortação da Guerra*.

The piece opens with a necromancer-priest telling the royal court of all his diabolical practices. After conjuring up two devils, Zebron and Danor, he has them fetch various figures from classical antiquity. The first is the beautiful Policena, daughter of Priam, suffering in Hell for having loved and having believed in love. She states what she deems the main qualities found in an ideal suitor: constancy, prudence, patience, and freedom. She goes on to praise warlike actions and warriors. Pentasileia, queen of the Amazons, follows and exhorts Portugal to war in verses that denote Vicente's ardent nationalism:

> Ó famoso Portugal,
> conhece teu bem profundo,
> pois até ó pólo segundo
> chega o teu poder real.
> Avante, avante, Senhores,
> pois com grandes favores
> todo o ceo vos favorece:
> ElRei de Fez esmorece,
> e Marrocos dá clamores.
>
> (4:147)

Achilles, Hannibal, Hector, and Scipio are all brought forward and enumerate the glories of Portugal, defender of the Faith. The author concludes the piece with a beautiful patriotic hymn sung by Hannibal.

The organic combination of philosophical dialogue, lofty symbolism, fantastic adventures, and underworld naturalism are common to the Menippea.

Bakhtin expands on this characteristic as follows:

A very important characteristic of the menippea is the organic combination within it of the free fantastic, the symbolic, at times even a mystical-religious element with an extreme and (from our point of view) crude *slum naturalism*. The adventures of truth on earth take place on the high road, in brothels, in the dens of thieves, in taverns, marketplaces, prisons, in the erotic orgies of secret cults, and so forth. The idea here fears no slum, is not afraid of any of life's filth. The man of the idea—the wise man—collides with worldly evil, depravity, baseness, and vulgarity in their most extreme expression. This slum naturalism is apparently already present in the earliest menippea. Of Bion Borysthenes the ancients were already saying that he "was the first to deck out philosophy in the motley dress of a hetaera." There is a great deal of slum naturalism in Varro and Lucian. But slum naturalism could develop to its broadest and fullest extent only in the menippea of Petronius and Apuleius. (*Dostoevsky*, 115)

In Vicentine plays, the naturalism associated with the dregs of society is not present in the extreme fashion of "worldly evil and depravity" found in the ancient Menippea. The reason may be that Master Gil produced drama primarily in accordance with the taste of an aristocratic audience to whom shocking degradation within the presentation was unacceptable under any pretext. But we must not infer that a mixture of the "high with the low" was altogether absent from the plays; quite the opposite: the idea, the truth—not necessarily the man of an idea—was confronted with a certain degree of baseness and a higher degree of vulgarity.

The relaxation of moral standards by many members of sixteenth-century Portuguese society was a great source of concern for our poet. Such concern manifests itself in his drama through the frequent inclusion of respected citizens who, though they stood to lose a great deal, allowed themselves to be overcome by their baser instincts. This left them exposed to those marginal individuals who thrived on the moral weaknesses of others. In *Farsa do Velho da Horta*, we come across an *homem honrado e muito rico, já velho* who instead of remaining loyal to his wife and position, falls ridiculously in love with a young girl. Unable to seduce her, he seeks the aid of a panderess named Branca Gil who is more interested in his money than in the fulfillment of his desires. The following conversation between the Old Man and the panderess is a fine example of contact between a wealthy individual and a representative of the dregs of society:

> *Vel.*   Venhais embora, minha amiga.
> *Bra.*   J'ela fica de bom jeito;
> mas pera isto andar direito,
> é razão que vo-lo diga.

Eu já, senhor meu, não posso
vencer uma moça tal
sem gastardes bem do vosso.
Vel. Eu lhe peitarei em grosso.
Bra. Hi está o feito nosso,
e não em al.
Perca-se toda a fazenda
por salvardes vossa vida.
Vel. Seja ela disso servida,
qu'escudada é mais contenda.
Bra. Deus vos ajude
e vos dê muita saúde,
que isso haveis de fazer:
que viola nem alaúde
nem quantos amores pude
não quer ver.
Remoçou-me'ela um brial
de seda e uns toucados.
Vel. Eis aqui trinta cruzados;
que lh'o façam mui real.

(5:169-70)

Here we grasp the precept that one must adhere to his hierarchical role in society lest, by adopting the vices of the *bas-fonds*, he fall prey to the amoral denizens of this environment.

Significantly, in the already-mentioned scene of the Fool coming to fetch the Old Man, the dialogue nicely illustrates the combination of lofty speech, on a tragic note, with the language of the common herd:

Par. Está a panela cozida,
minha dona quer jentar:
não quereis?
Vel. Não hei-de comer, que me pês,
nem quero comer bocado.
Par. E se vós, dono, morreis?
Então depois não falareis,
senão finado.

Então na terra nego jazer,
então finar dono estendido.
Vel. Ó quem não fora nacido,
ou acabasse de viver!
Par. Assi, pardeus.
Então tanta pulga em vós,
tanta bichoca nos olhos,
ali c'os finados sós;

e comer-vos-ão a vós
os piolhos.

Comer-vos-ão as cigarras,
e os sapos morreré, morreré.

(5:153)

This is essentially a parody of the tragic speech of the love-
stricken heroes of chivalric novels along with a role reversal. By
introducing a fool with little education, accustomed to physical labor
and incapable of discerning the Old Man's predicament, Gil Vicente
has created a parodic double, whose sole purpose is to "discrown its
counterpart." The loss of appetite and the desire to die were
trademarks of a knight doing penance over his rejection by a damsel,
a common device in the tradition of *amour courtois*. To the Fool,
such depravation was inconceivable, for its result was death. The
naturalistic description of what happens to a lifeless body once it is
buried is meant to bring the Old Man to his senses. There is, as it
were, a reversal of roles: the Fool, because of his pragmatism before
the necessities of life, becomes less foolish and more judicious
(crowned); the Old Man, on the other hand, by ridiculously pursuing
the favors of a young girl and by behaving like a novelistic knight
when rejected by the girl, takes on all the characteristics associated
with fools (discrowned).

Much the same occurs in *Floresta de Enganos*, where a learned
doctor, in spite of his age, becomes enamored of a young girl of
modest means. She takes advantage of the old man's love and
makes a complete fool of him. As previously mentioned, she makes
him dress as a woman and sift flour, to the disbelief of an old lady
who discovers him. Notice the vulgar language employed by the girl
and old lady in this scene:

Moç.   Não vêdes, dona, esta perra
        o negro geito que tem?
Vel.   Peneirai, má ora, bem,
        que não sois nova na terra.
        Hui, cadelinha,
        onde jeitas a farinha?
        Não queres falar, cadella?
        Esta pelle de toninha
        olho mao se meteo nella.
Dou.   Porque vós, mia Señora,
        estar tanto destemplada?
        Ya tudo estar peneirada:
        que bradar comigo aora?

> Que cosa estar vos hablando?
> Á mi llama Caterina Furnando,
> nunca a mí cadella não.
Vel. Seu dali tómo hum tição...
> e vós estais patorneando?
> Olhade a mal entrouxada!
> Ó almadraque bolorento!

> (3:196-97)

The adventure takes place in a dingy room where the doctor —not necessarily the wise man—is confronted with the extreme expression of vulgarity. The idea enacted—or rather, converted to dialogue—is that of Gil Vicente attempting to convey the ridiculousness of the doctor's position. The predicament that the doctor has created for himself is such that, if his hope of seducing the girl is to remain alive, he must lie to the point of making a total ass of himself: "á mí llama Caterina Furnando." Master Gil's philosophy is here decked out "in the multi-colored dress" not of the hetaera but of the doctor.

Clérigo da Beira is a piece in which free fantasy is combined with underworld naturalism to meet an objective other than truth. In it, a priest goes hunting rabbits on Christmas Eve. His son, a brat by the name of Francisco, accompanies him. At his father's request, he unwillingly returns home to fetch a ferret that had been left behind. Meanwhile, Gonçalo, a peasant's son, appears with a hare and two capons, which are stolen from him by two courtiers. The priest promises to help retrieve the stolen animals and warns Gonçalo of a Negro thief, who immediately shows up speaking broken Portuguese. He wins Gonçalo's confidence by engaging him in conversation and, while the naive youth bathes in the river, makes off with his hat, belt, and sack. An old lady appears, accompanied by a girl named Cezília, who is possessed by the spirit of one Pedreanes. Cezília reveals the identity of the courtly thieves who robbed Gonçalo. These two, having reappeared, ask her to foretell the future of the courtly members of the audience.

As deduced from this summary, the adventure, which unfolds entirely on the road, contains more than its share of naturalistic scenes. Naturalism goes so far as to pervade Pedreanes's predictions, offered through his medium Cezília, concerning Gonçalo's marital status:

> Casarás polo Natal
> com mulher sem tua perda;
> seu corpo como cristal,
> e achar-lhe-ás um sinal

no meio da coxa esquerda.
E tem na teta direita
um lũar com três cabelos;
pola cinta muito estreita,
de uma nádega contreita,
e zambra dos cotovelos.

(6:33)

It is difficult to pinpoint the precise object of this play. It
appears as though Gil Vicente had a clear-cut idea of his direction
when he began to elaborate the plot, but some unexpected exigency
forced him to change course and conclude the piece in such a weak
fashion, from a dramatic point of view. Óscar de Pratt sheds some
light on this subject:

A cena final, em que a velha apresenta a demoninhada Cezília, é apenas
um episódio de remate, na efabulação da peça, que visava a desmascarar
os dois vaganaus. Prevê-se, porém, que quase no final da composição é
que o autor teve a ideia de aproveitar o ensejo para fazer graciosas
alusões a corte. Tanto à cena se afasta, finalmente, do assunto da peça
que o argumento, aliás minucioso, não cita este pormenor.[14]

Another piece in which the religious element is mixed with crude
naturalism is *Auto dos Físicos*, whose opening scene shows a lovesick
priest ordering his servant Perico to pay a visit on Blanca Denisa.
Perico is to hand her a letter containing the priest's declaration of
love. Because on a previous visit she had threatened to beat the
servant should he return with any messages from the priest, the
following conversation ensues between servant and master:

Clé.   Não veis vos?
Moç.   Bem o vejo
que não vos quer sóis olhar.
Clé.   Caza mata el porfiar,
como dice el refran viejo.
Moç.   Diz que me há-de esbofetar.
Clé.   Aunque ella eso diga...
Moç.   Pior o há-de fazer.
Quando ela bom vos quiser,
que me pinguem na barriga.
Clé.   Vé, háceme este placer.

Moç.   Dizê vós missa primeiro.
Clé.   Cuerpo de Dios con la misa,
y con el mozo y con la prisa!

(6:98)

We have here a striking example of familiarization, naturalism (profanation and mention of bodily parts), oxymoronic combination (*mésalliance*), bringing-down-to-earth or debasement, and symbolism—a rather exaggerated fragment of what constitutes a thoroughly carnivalized genre. The irreverence demonstrated by the servant in his replies to the priest produces an atmosphere of familiarization; this familiarized atmosphere, in turn, is the result of the *mésalliance* created once the priest took on the servant as a confidant. The latter's preoccupation with corporal punishment has a debasing effect on the priest: he grows steadily more impatient with the boy's apparent lack of obedience and practically begs him to go and do as directed. At his wits' end, the priest explodes with a profane exclamation when the servant asks that he say mass before any message is delivered.

Observe the symbolic significance of the oxymoronic combination "religiosity/secularity": the priest, having strayed from his religious path (the desire to break the vows of celibacy), has placed himself in a position where the servant must remind him of his supposed principal concern, the saying of mass. This episode symbolizes the Church, which by ignoring its original purpose, finds itself the target of the layman's (Gil Vicente's) constructive criticism. So frequently did Master Gil make the Church the object of his criticism that he has often been referred to as a proselyte of Erasmus.

The last scene of *Triunfo do Inverno*, a scene that could have been developed into a separate play entitled *Triunfo do Verão*, presents an unexpected mixture of free fantasy with the baseness and vulgarity of the *lumpenproletariat*.

The figure of Spring enters and reveals why it should eavesdrop on the conversation between a blacksmith and his wife, a baker:

> Aquel maestro herrero
> tiene la muger hornera,
> y quieren (lo que Dios no quiera)
> que siempre sea genero.
> Tiéneme amenazado,
> porque los hago sudar;
> yo tengo de los escuchar,
> que es casal muy concertado.
>
> (4:318)

The blacksmith and his wife start to argue and parody the *Romance de la Bela Mal Maridada*.[15] The couple's language is laden with profanities. For example:

> *For.*   Chouricinho engargueijado,
> forunço de gata prenhe,
> não sei, marido coitado,
> se te venda, se tempenhe.
> Pois não prestas pera nada
> quero-me quitar de ti;
> que a bella mal empregada
> se pôde dizer por mi.
>
> (4:320)

Their argument is interrupted by the figure of the Sintra mountainrange who, appalled by a negative remark of the blacksmith against Spring, exclaims:

> Hũa forneira pelada,
> e hum ferreiro pelado
> terem coração ousado
> com lingoa escomugada
> falar no Verão sagrado!
>
> (4:321)

The blacksmith and wife enumerate why they dislike this particular season. The figure of Spring then intercedes and remarks:

> Disputar no es cosa honesta
> con horneras ni herreros;
> porque bien caro les cuesta,
> en mi tiempo, sus dineros,
> trabajados por la siesta.
>
> (4:323-24)

Unlike most medieval poems that dealt with the contrasting pleasures of Winter and Spring, the point of this play is to suggest their hardships.[16] With Spring, it was difficult to find persons to whom this season was displeasing, because it is universally a time for rejoicing. However, because of the nature of the work performed, certain lowly occupations became more difficult during the warmer months. The vulgar invectives heaped on Spring by the blacksmith and his baker-wife were a direct result of their lowly professions. The naturalistic is here juxtaposed with the lofty for the purpose of testing the truism: one man's delight is another man's inconvenience.

Syncrisis is widely employed in the Menippea.

In the Menippea, the *pro et contra* of the ultimate questions of life, those with an ethico-practical inclination, are laid bare. As Bakhtin explains:

> Boldness of invention and the fantastic element are combined in the menippea with an extraordinary philosophical universalism and a capacity to contemplate the world on the broadest possible scale. The menippea is a genre of "ultimate questions." In it ultimate philosophical positions are put to the test. The menippea strives to provide, as it were, the ultimate and decisive words and acts of a person, each of which contains the whole man, the whole of his life in its entirety. This feature of the genre was apparently especiallly prominent in the early menippea (in Heraclides Ponticus, Bion, Teles, and Menippus), but it has been preserved, although sometimes in weakened form, as the characteristic feature in all varieties of the genre. Under menippean conditions the very nature and process of posing philosophical problems, as compared with the Socratic dialogue, had to change abruptly: all problems that were in the least "academic" (gnoseological and aesthetic) fell by the wayside, complex and extensive modes of argumentation also fell away, and there remained essentially only naked "ultimate questions" with an ethical and practical bias. Typical for the menippea is syncrisis (that is, juxtaposition) of precisely such stripped-down "ultimate positions in the world." (*Dostoevsky*, 115-16)

The syncritic device in the Socratic dialogue, though Bakhtin does not say so here, is a direct result of the dialogical nature of truth. In order to arrive at the truth of any given concept, all thoughts or points of view concerning that concept have to be verbalized and counterposed. Any weak or fallacious idea is thus exposed and discarded. The method used to elicit each opinion is "anacrisis," best defined as "the provocation of the word by the word." In the Menippea, however, such provocation was a result of the plot situation and not of the interlocutor's questioning (as in the Socratic dialogue). Whether provoked by plot or interlocutor, the truth does not originate from nor lodge in an individual's mind; it arises from the dialogical exchange of people collectively searching for the truth. It was the bringing together of people for the purpose of dialogically establishing the truth that compelled Socrates to refer to himself as a "panderer."

As Bakhtin points out, the Menippea seeks to give rise to fundamental questions concerning the application of knowledge on a moral basis. Questions of knowledge for its own sake and of aesthetic principles are perforce excluded as outside the realm of satire. Hence, the writer of Menippea must dispense with any epistemological concerns and debate, through his heroes, the pros and cons of society's moral issues. Vicentine plot action often entails a dialogized confrontation between two or more individuals intended to alert the audience to the diverse points on a given matter. In *Auto da História de Deus*, boldness of invention is masterfully combined with syncretism to produce a concise summary of the Old Testament culminating in the resurrection of Christ.

The appearance of Job in Limbo leads to a fine illustration of syncrisis, as these fragments of the conversation between him and Satan demonstrate:

Job.   Se os bens do mundo nos dá a ventura,
também em ventura está quem os tem.
O bem que é mudavel não pode ser bem,
mas mal, pois é causa de tanta tristura;
e se Deus os dá,
como eu creio mui bem que será,
e a fortuna tem tanto poder,
que os tira logo cada vez que quer,
o segredo disto, oh! quem m'o dirá,
pera o eu saber?

Sat.   Falemos um pouco, Job, a de parte
sobre esse segredo, verás que te digo.
. . . .
Deus é aquele que trata assi;
quer-te gran mal e diz mal de ti:
não cures dele, e logo tornarás
a como te vi.
Tu dás com teus males louvores a Deus,
e ele pesa-lhe por tu noméa-lo:
renega, renega de ser seu vassalo,
e logo verás tecer outros véus.

Job.   Se o eu leixar,
qual é o senhor que m'há d'emparar?
Qual é o Deus que me pode valer?
Nos bens desta vida não está o perder,
que assi como assi cá hão-de ficar,
pois hei-de morrer.
Eu creio, Mundo, que o meu Redentor
vive, e no dia mais derradeiro
eu o verei Redentor verdadeiro,
meu Deus, meu Senhor e meu Salvador.
Eu o verei, eu,
não outrem por mim, nem com olho seu,
mas o meu olho, assim como está;
porque minha carne se levantará,
e em carne mea verei o Deus meu,
que me salvará.

(2:190-91)

The ethico-practical question put forth here is that though human beings endure a great deal of suffering in this world, such travails are merely temporary and we must resign ourselves to them regardless of whether God is responsible. Succumbing to temptation so as to alleviate our misery only precludes salvation. We sinners will eventually come before God, must answer to him, and place in his wisdom our eternal fate.

By accepting God as an omnipotent figure and by resigning himself to his mundane tribulations, Job is able to face death with the optimistim denied the atheist. Job's words, before his departure from the world of the living, embody all his previous decisive actions and express his ultimate philosophical stand (the *pro*), which runs counter to Satan's fallacious argument (the *contra*):

> Oh! bento e louvado seja o meu senhor!
> O que ele me mandar
> a vida é sua, pode-a tirar,
> a morte é nossa de juro e herdade;
> e pois que ele é o juiz da verdade
> faça-se logo sem mais dilatar
> a sua vontade.
>
> (2:193-94)

Further on, the question that Moses asks King David is answered by the allegorical figure of Death. The response embodies an irrefutable truth, an ultimate conclusion—man is dust and to dust he shall return:

> *Moi.*   Senhor Rei David, não tendes na corte
> cirurgiães e físicos mores,
> astrólogos grandes e muito doctores,
> que vos dem saúde e livrem da morte?
> *Mor.*   Olhai, não vai nisso;
> o mal que se cura não é mal de siso.
> Andam deitando remendos à vida;
> mas quanto ao despejo, pois não tens guarida,
> lembra-te, homem, com muito aviso
> que és terra podrida.
>
> (2:199)

To the naive and somewhat arrogant belief of the character Moses, that death can be avoided by scientific expertise procured by power and wealth, the author, speaking through Death, juxtaposes the irremediable destiny of earthly beings. Be that as it may, the words are directed beyond the audience; here, as in most mystery plays, the word rings out before heaven and earth, i.e., before the entire world.

Such syncrisis of stripped-bare ultimate positions in the piece led Jack H. Parker to comment:

> The audience assembled to be edified on the occasion of the play's debut surely did receive, in a manner vigorously conceived and executed, a recapitulation of theological history in capsule form and many lessons on which to ponder.[17]

One play in which the entire action evolves around the constant confrontation of opposing viewpoints is *Auto da Sibila Cassandra*, for the plot is marked by cutting dialogical syncrises: humility versus arrogance, matrimony versus spinsterhood. Cassandra's obstinacy, her absolute disdain toward marriage, arise from the "crisis vision" theme so common in carnivalized literatures. Through a dream or premonition, Cassandra sees "with her own eyes" the possibility of a radically different human existence on earth. This vision influences her reality-testing to such a degree that to her the most preposterous aspiration—to be chosen mother of Christ—seems perfectly within reason.

The belief in a sort of rebirth or renewal is already well imbedded in Cassandra's psyche at the outset of the piece. Her objection on different grounds to Solomon's marriage proposal attests to this; for though Cassandra lists the many negative characteristics of husbands she has observed, in a previous statement she makes it clear that "no quiero ser desposada / ni casada, / ni monja ni ermitaña" (1:53). From this statement one can deduce that Cassandra must be awaiting a certain extraordinary event in her life: with marriage out of the question, the only option left to a spinster was to enter a convent or become a recluse. Nevertheless, Cassandra, in making her anti-marital views known, subtly reveals that a spinster's life is not what she has in mind.

Later, when her aunts, the prophetesses Erutea, Peresica, and Cimeria, intercede on Solomon's behalf, the pros and cons of marriage continue to be tossed around, with Cassandra again twice insinuating that she is saving herself for a purpose she is hesitant to reveal. These are the two insinuations:

> *Cim.* Tu madre eu [sic] su testamento
> (no te miento)
> manda que cases, que es bueno.
> *Cas.* Otro casamiento ordeno
> en mi seno.

. . . .

Per.   Si tu madre eso hiciera!...
Cas.   Bien, qué fuera?
Per.   Nunca tú fueras nacida.
Cas.   Yo quiero ser escogida
        en otra vida,
        de mas perfeta manera.

(1:58-59)

Cassandra's uncles, the prophets Isaiah, Moses, and Abraham, then call upon her in an attempt to succeed where the aunts have failed. Cassandra, however, is inflexible in her decision to remain single.

Suddenly, after mentioning that she is aware God will be incarnate and a virgin will bear him, Cassandra shocks everyone by revealing the real reason she refuses to marry: she believes that she is to be the chosen virgin. Naturally, such revelation terminates the exposition of the pros and cons of marriage, up to that point the focus of the play. The revelation gives rise to the second syncritical exposition: arrogance versus humility.

Immediately after Cassandra's disclosure, both aunts and uncles begin to call upon scriptural and apocryphal prophecies to dissuade the foolish girl; Uncle Isaiah, one of the first to address her, introduces the second dramatical syncrisis:

> Cállate loca perdida,
> que desa madre escogida
> otra cosa se escrevió.
>
>   Tú eres della al revés
> si bien ves:
> porque tú eres humosa,
> soberbia y presuntuosa,
> que es la cosa
> que mas desviada es.
> La madre de Dios sin par,
> es de notar,
> que humildosa ha de nacer,
> y humildosa conceber,
> y humildosa ha de criar.

(1:71)

From this point, the dialogue is structured to belie Cassandra's presumptuous aspiration by stressing how humble Christ's mother must be in accordance with the prophecies. Toward the play's conclusion, fantasy is used to substantiate the foretelling of Christ's birth from a humble virgin: curtains are drawn and the entire Nativity scene appears before Solomon, Cassandra, and her aunts and uncles. Cassandra, realizing her mistake, praises the true Virgin and thus comes to her senses.

Summing up, we may say that in this play, two ethico-practical questions are put to the test: marriage versus spinsterhood and humility versus arrogance. It appears that in regard to the first, Master Gil was on the side of marriage; though his character Cassandra gives good reasons why a maiden should remain so, none of these is her reason for shunning Solomon. Aspiring to bear Christ, she abstains from matrimony. It is not that Cassandra is opposed to marriage but that she feels obliged to give that impression in order to conceal her real desire: to be the Virgin. One is left with the impression that woman's maternal instinct will always seek marriage regardless of any indisposition toward the institution itself. After all, was Cassandra not choosing God as her spouse?

Once Cassandra's presumptuous ambition becomes known, marriage assumes secondary importance. Her belief that she will be chosen conflicts with prophecies that indicate that Christ's mother, whose name will be Mary, will be known for her humility, among other fine qualities. The prophecies are then recounted by the characters and with the appearance of the Nativity scene, humility (the *pro* of this ethical question) triumphs over arrogance (the *contra*). The syncrisis is inserted to convey the playwright's moral message: Christian qualities and not social status—Mary's origins are as humble as Cassandra's—are what is relevant in the kingdom of God. Anacrisis, as in the Menippea, is here plot-borne and not originated by an interlocutor or a chorus as was customary in classical drama.

Before concluding this section, we must examine what is not only a fine illustration of syncrisis, but also perhaps the most often-cited example of Vicentine social criticism. This, of course, is the scene in *Auto da Lusitânia* where Everyman, a symbolic figure dressed in the attire of a rich merchant, comes across Nobody, a poor soul who asks him:

> Nin. Como hás nome cavaleiro?
> Tod. Eu hei nome Todo o Mundo
>   e meu tempo todo inteiro
>   sempre é buscar dinheiro,
>   e sempre nisto me fundo.

(6:84)

Everyman symbolizes the *sacra fames auri*, the vulgar crowd with its lowly instincts that reduce life to the search for money, honors, praise, pleasures, well-being, flattery, etc.; Everyman is the greedy, selfish, ambitious man who seeks out others not for what they are, but for what they appear to be (the *contra*).

> *Nin.*   Eu hei nome *Ninguém*
> e busco a consciência.
>
> (6:84)

Nobody is the humble, honest, and righteous man who seeks out conscience, virtue, reprehension, honesty, truth, and sincerity (the *pro*).

Thus, a syncritical dialogue is established between representatives of those two worlds discussed in Gil Vicente's letter to his monarch, King John III: the one of the truth, or the first world, and the other of falsehood, or the second world. Interesting observations are made by Jack E. Tomlins with respect to this duality in the letter which is, after all, the *pro et contra* of earthly existence:

> Gil Vicente presents a two-faced mirror of man. In his letter, he primarily notes the nature of this world... a vast composition of opposites: the good and perfect and the evil and imperfect. The imperfect "is" (the imperfect nature of man after the Original Sin) always points to the perfect "ought to be" (man as he was originally after his creation by God). This is the idea of man in popular farce, man in his daily existence. While Gil Vicente, in his religious drama, succeeded in creating a sort of lesser humor from the shepherd's ignorance and simplicity before the Nativity manger, he evinced the court's revelry in his farces, where man's imperfection is always obvious vis-à-vis that nature of man as he ought to be were he perfect; this "ought to be" is never far below the surface. These recurring themes (not dramatic per se and representing the expression of the interaction of opposites in the pieces) create unity in Gil Vicente's religious and burlesque plays, and provide a fitting explanation for his drama, which, for so long, has been an enigma to scholars.[18]

The Menippea often relies on a trilevel structure: Earth, Heaven, and Hell.

In accordance with Bakhtin, the philosophical universalism of the Menippea appears in a trilevel construction: action and dialogical syncrisis are transferred from earth to Olympus and to the nether world. The earlier mentioned *Apocolocyntosis* of Seneca is a work in which such transfer is made with considerable external evidence.

In it, further "threshold dialogues" are delivered with considerable external clearness, at the gates of Olympus (where Claudius was denied admission), and on the threshold of the infernal regions.

The Menippea's trilevel construction exercised a decisive influence on the analogous construction of the medieval mystery play and its scenery. The "threshold dialogue" genre took hold and was widely disseminated throughout the Middle Ages in serious and comical genres alike; it enjoyed vast popularity during the Reformation, as the literature of this period indicates, in the so-called "literature of the heavenly gates." Increasingly, the representation of the infernal regions became more important in the Menippea, begetting the special genre of the "dialogue of the dead" so common in Renaissance European literature of the seventeenth and eighteenth centuries.

Because Gil Vicente stood at the crossroads of two ages, the medieval and the humanistic, it is not surprising that the literary trends of both are found in his work. The *Trilogia das Barcas*, three plays or scenes closely resembling the trilevel construction of the ancient Menippea, has been linked, though not conclusively, to Lucian's *Dialogues of the Dead* by Paulo Quintela, who has completed one of the most thorough studies concerning the origins of this trilogy. He speculates:

> Resta considerar—o que até hoje, que eu saiba, ainda se não fez—o caso da tradição lucianesca. Tudo o que sobre este assunto vou dizer aventuro-o como pura hipótese, pois me faltam os fundamentos da tradição medieval dos *Diálogos dos Mortos*. A leitura do décimo Diálogo de Luciano, Caronte, Hermes e diferentes Mortos, e sobretudo a de *A chegada aos Infernos ou o Tirano*, são tão impressionantes, para quem se preocupe com on nosso tema, que de facto se não pode deixar de pôr a questão da possibilidade de Gil Vicente, por qualquer via, ter chegado ao seu conhecimento.[19]

Indeed, in both these dialogized stories, there are striking similarities to the *Trilogia das Barcas*. In the second story of Lucian's account, the tyrant Megapenthes, about to embark on Charon's barge, en route to Hades, beseeches Klotho to allow him to return to the world of the living for the ensuing purposes:

> Mooress! I am not asking for much time! Allow me at least this day to instruct my wife somewhat about the money and where I buried the big treasure![20]

This reminds us of the tyrant nobleman's request to the devil in the *Barca do Inferno*:

> Mas esperai vós aqui;
> tornarei à outra vida
> ver minha dama querida,
> que se quer matar por mi.

(2:46)

As in the *Barca do Inferno*, there is also a cobbler who makes the journey to the beyond in the ferryboat. His presence embodies the author's conviction that social distinctions are eradicated by death (the cobbler crosses the Styx on the shoulders of the tyrant king).

Aubrey Bell shares Quintela's opinion when he observes that "there are passages in the *Barcas* which are not altogether unworthy of their remote ancestors—the *Frogs* of Aristophanes or the *Dialogues* of Lucian."[21] Eugenio Asensio also acknowledges Lucian's Dialogues as a likely source in the composition of the *Barcas*, but censures Quintela for neglecting other possible sources.[22]

The reader should at this point be reminded of not only the carnival traits encountered in our discussion of *The Frogs*, but also of Bakhtin's remark: "The fullest picture of the genre is of course provided by the Menippean satires of Lucian, which have come down to us intact (although not representing all varieties of the genre)" (*Dostoevsky*, 113). Certainly, the most striking tendencies of the Menippea—to satirize and moralize—are found as the main ingredients in all of Lucian's *Dialogues*. In this sense, it could be deduced that Lucian serves as a link between the original Menippea and the Vicentine drama, although we should not assume that the Portuguese dramatist was familiar with Lucian's work; the Menippea and all its related genres are literary manifestations of a carnival attitude that developed because of the powerful influence that Western man's seasonal festivities exerted over him. Menippus and Lucian, as well as Gil Vicente, were only a few among the many aesthetic exponents of an enduring popular view that is prevalent even in this century, e.g., in the Brazilian modernist Mário de Andrade.[23]

Returning to the trilevel construction in the Vicentine trilogy, we observe that the ships of Heaven and Hell, with their respective boatmen—the Devil with his assistant and the Angel—await the approaching souls. Purgatory, though one of the three plays is entitled *A Barca do Purgatório*, is not represented by any ship since, as it turns out, Purgatory is not a destination in the trilogy, but the point of departure itself.[24]

Each ship is in itself a threshold: he who climbs aboard automatically enters the region of his merited destination. The conversations between the passing souls and the boatmen are "threshold dialogues"; in them the deceased's decisive words and actions, each containing his or her entire life and morality, are laid bare. In the following fragment from the *Barca do Inferno*, a priest reveals to the Devil his reason for not embarking on the Hell-bound ship:

Dia.   Que é isso, Padre? que vai lá?
Fra.   *Deo gratias!* Sam cortezão.
Dia.   Sabeis também o tordião?
Fra.   É mal que m'esquecerá.
Dia.   Essa dama há-de entrar cá?
Fra.   Não sei onde embarcarei.
Dia.   Ela é vossa?
Fra.   Eu não sei;
por minha a trago eu cá.

Dia.   E não vos punham lá grosa,
nesse convento sagrado?
Fra.   Assi fui bem açoutado.
Dia.   Que cousa tão preciosa!
Entrai, Padre reverendo.
Fra.   Pera onde levais gente?
Dia.   Pera aquele fogo ardente,
que não temeste vivendo.

Fra.   Juro a Deus que não t'entendo:
e este hábito não me val?
Dia.   Gentil padre mundanal,
a Berzebu vos encomendo.
Fra.   Corpo de Deus consagrado!
Pola fé de Jesu Cristo,
qu'eu não posso entender isto:
eu hei de ser condenado?
    Um padre tão namorado,
e tanto dado à virtude!
Assi Deus me dê saúde,
que estou maravilhado.

(2:57-59)

By bringing his mistress with him and not being at all ashamed of his dalliance, the priest reminds us of the friar in the *Auto das Fadas* who delivered the burlesque sermon on the Vergilian line *omnia vincit amor*. Like that friar, who had been condemned to Hell for weakness of the flesh, the priest here seems to be of the impression that he has committed no sin; on the contrary, to love is human and, as such, should be regarded as normal and vouchsafed the acceptance of God. Therefore, his carnal desire is justified. That he was flogged while alive for having loved seems, in his opinion, satisfactory atonement if, perchance, to love is indeed sinful.

Realizing that his amorous life has earned him eternal damnation, the priest desperately mentions his most favorable point in order to gain salvation: he is, after all, a man of the cloth. This has no effect on the Devil who entrusts him to Beelzebub. In despair and amazement, the cleric expounds a philosophical stance that reveals him entire: a lovesick priest who earnestly believes that he has been virtuous and is extremely perplexed at his damnation, because he expected salvation all along.

This is the selfsame carnival logic, so prevalent in the Menippea, of an impostor's "elevation" (the priest's pleasures and expectations while in the world of the living), his comical "discrowning" by the whole folk on the square (the Devil's ironic remarks that serve to awaken the priest to his own unpromising reality), and his "downward" fall (his eternal damnation).

Throughout this trilogy, "threshold" acquires the meaning of a pivotal "point" in which crisis, radical change, or an unexpected turn of events takes place, where decisions are made, where demarcation lines are crossed, where souls are saved or damned.

The Fool in the *Barca do Inferno*, having shied away from the Hell-bound ship and its pilot, approaches the Heaven-bound ship and says to the Angel:

Par.	Ou da barca!
Anj.	Tu que queres?
Par.	Quereis-me passar além?
Anj.	Quem és tu?
Par.	Não sou ninguém.
Anj.	Tu passarás, se quiseres.
	Porque em todos teus fazeres,
	per malícia não erraste;
	tua simpreza t'abaste
	pera gozar dos prazeres.

(2:54)

This threshold dialogue depicts not only a decision made by the Angel as to the Fool's destination, but also an unexpected turn of events: the reader or spectator would expect the Fool, given the obscene insults he has heaped on the Devil, to have no recourse but to embark on the Hell-bound ship, having been turned away by the

Angel for his amorality; however, he is saved, for he acts not from malice but from poverty of spirit. Sebastião Pestana furnishes us with a most poetical interpretation of the Fool's role in the scene:

> Para Gil Vicente e para o Povo, o "Parvo" é o "pobre de espírito", aquele a quem o dulcíssimo Rabi da Galileia, no Seu extraordinário (porque é divino) "Sermão da Montanha", não deixou de lançar um pouco de luz intensa de Seus olhos melancólicos, não negou o amparo da Sua boca suavíssima e até estreitou no Seu amplíssimo coração, numa hora de amargura, juntamente com todos os que entrariam no Reino dos Céus.[25]

Next appear, in order, the cobbler and priest previously mentioned, a panderess by the name of Brizida Vaz, a Jew who tries to bribe the Angel, a magistrate with some tirades in Latin, a prosecutor, and a hanged man. The beach where the ships are about to depart takes on the characteristics of the carnival square. As in this festive spot, representatives of all earthly roles come together on equal terms and enter into familiar contact; in death, all who wore crowns in life are discrowned. In the Menippean trilevel presentation or, as it were, device, the carnival logic of a topsy-turvy world was often applied. It was not at all unusual that an emperor became a slave and vice versa. As noted in the *Barca do Inferno*, the Fool, typifying one of society's lowest members, is saved while others from the highest echelons are condemned. There are, however, exceptions to this carnival inversion, such as the four knights of the Order of Christ who, at the conclusion of the piece, are saved for having died in holy war. Master Gil's patriotism, so significant throughout his entire corpus, would not allow him to deride or carnivalize his monarchs' policies. It may also be that his total dependency on these rulers was a limiting influence on his satirical targets. In his Introduction to the *Comédia de Rubena*, Giuseppe Tavani explains that:

> When we speak of expressive freedom in Vicentine drama, we need to recognize, above all, its restraints. Gil Vicente is the court's leading comic poet, and, at its service, he portrays its activity: as with all courtly poets therefore, his expressive freedom is limited because of the special audience's likes and dislikes, refinement and crudeness.[26]

Yet in this trilogy, all in all, people from varying social ranks, gathered on the beach to have their fates determined, are made equal by death and are equal in the eyes of the boatmen. Their behavior on the beach before the boatmen corresponds to the roles they played in ordinary life, i.e., they are either haughty, picaresque, vulgar, or insolent in keeping with their earthly demeanor. Soon, though, all come to the realization that the atmosphere of death is one of sudden and unexpected changes of fate, of instantaneous rises and falls, of "crownings and discrownings." The dead are suddenly struck by the criticalness of the situation and feel that they are on the "threshold." The encounter with the boatmen is irrefutably a most special moment for these souls—here a matter of seconds or minutes decides either a blissful or a tortured eternity. The exposition by each soul of his or her ultimate position is an attempt to gain passage to the desired destination (Heaven). However, it is the weighing of the *pro et contra* of each individual position that allows the Angel to reach a fair decision with regard to each soul's terminus.

Bahktin mentions that the carnivalization of the nether world in the Menippea was most influential on the medieval tradition of a "happy hell," the culmination of which is the works of Rabelais. The frivolous exchange of ideas in the nether world of antiquity and the Christian hell is typical of this medieval tradition; in the mystery plays of this age both hell and devil are consistently carnivalized.

Such assertions do not seem to apply to the representation of the infernal regions in Vicentine drama. The devil (hell, though often mentioned, is never directly represented) is repeatedly portrayed as a sort of harmless jester, but never are we allowed to forget that behind his comical façade lurks the torment of the regions over which he rules supreme. These lines spoken by the devil in the *Barca da Glória* give succinct testimony of this:

> Mirad, Señor, por iten
> os tengo acá en mi rol,
> y habeis de pasar allen.
> Veis aquellos fuegos bien?
> allí se coge la frol.
>
> Veis aquel gran fumo espeso,
> que sale daquellas peñas?
> Allí perdereis el vueso,
> y mas, Señor, os confieso
> que habeis de mensar las greñas.

(2:130)

In spite of the fact that only the *Trilogia das Barcas* offers a clear-cut depiction of the exemplary medieval "threshold dialogue" genre, this does not imply that it was the only Vicentine piece evincing the influence of the "dialogue of the dead," a special genre that would reach its apogee during the Renaissance. The prologue of the *Auto da Feira*, delivered by Mercury, brings to mind some of the techniques of this genre. In the words of Marques Braga:

> Como nos "Diálogos dos Mortos" do clássico grego Luciano e no *Diálogo de Mercurio y Carón* (1528) de Alfonso de Valdés também no Prólogo deste *Auto [da Feira]*, Mercúrio, figura principal, contempla a vida e costumes dos homens e "chasqueia da astrologia" que se tornara uma superstição dos homens cultos de 1500. (1:195)

There appears in the Menippea a special type of "experimental fantasticality," totally alien to the antique epos and tragedy.

Bakhtin observes that, under the definite influence of the Menippea, this line of experimental fantasticality continued, in the centuries after Lucian and Apuleius, in Rabelais, Swift, Voltaire, and others.

The myriad of fantastic elements employed by Master Gil in the construction of his pieces is ample testimony that our poet fittingly belongs on the list. His work reflects one of the most inventive and prodigious minds of occidental dramaturgy.

Over the course of this chapter time and time again we have observed the inclusion of Christian fantasticality (devils, angels, miracles, apparitions, etc.) to achieve the desired satire and/or syncrisis. Yet we have not touched upon another realm of fantasticality frequently exploited by Gil Vicente: the traditional and popular supernatural.

With regard to this brand of experimental fantasticality, António J. Saraiva and Óscar Lopes affirm:

> Movimentando uma população fantástica de mitos tradicionais ou imaginados por ele próprio, Gil Vicente cria verdadeiros poemas encenados, revelando-se um extraordinário poeta de tipo pouco freqüente na literatura portuguesa, não introvertido, à maneira de Bernardim Ribeiro, antes aberto a inesgotável e pluriforme beleza do vasto mundo, cuja expressão mais, típica se encontra nos *Triunfos* das estações: *Auto dos Quatro Tempos* e, sobretudo, *Triunfo do Inverno*, personificado num portentoso João da Grenha, que assume, em admirável friso de metáforas, toda a épica grandeza dos elementos em fúria.... Esta inspiração insinua-se também nos autos cavaleirescos (por. ex. *D. Duardos*), nas farsas (*Quem Tem Farelos?*) e "tragicomédias" (*Comédia de Rubena, Auto da Lusitânia*). Pode dizer-se que no teatro vicentino cristaliza certo foclore peninsular, enriquecido com a dupla herança da mitologia clássica, da literatura bíblica, e ainda com a contribuição dos romances de cavalaria e dos rimances castelhanos, então

em voga na corte.[27]

In the *Comédia de Rubena,* a sorceress and three fairies (supernatural characters from traditional folk tales) are instrumental in the development of its fantastic plot. Prior to the composition of this comedy, however, Gil Vicente had introduced these magical characters in a farce with the appropriate title of *Auto das Fadas.* This farce provides a prime example of boundless fantasticality within a theatrical piece.

The *Auto das Fadas* derides the common belief (prevalent even among the nobility) in the supernatural power of sorcerers. Genebra Pereira, a sorceress fearing that "a prendessem por usar de seu oficio," arrives at court. She describes her aims before the royal family: to take pity on ill-wed women, to help a disillusioned lover, to arrange marriages, etc. Then she produces a bowl and a black sack containing various ingredients. Aided by these artifacts and chanting some mumbo-jumbo, Genebra attempts to conjure the devil.

A devil does appear and the sorceress orders him to bring forth three marine fairies. The devil, who speaks in Picardese, misunderstands her and brings back two friars from Hell (*fadas-frailes*). After a burlesque sermon on *amor omnia vincit* by one of the friars, the devil returns with the requested fairies. In the traditional manner of all fairies, these read the fate of all those attending the presentation: the royal family first, then the nobility.

What was the playwright's purpose in bringing together supernatural fictional characters and actual spectators? Óscar de Pratt supplies this plausible reason:

> Suponho que foi por ocasião de uma mais intensa acção repressora (contra as práticas ocultas) que Gil Vicente teria encontrado ensejo para a composição desta farsa, na qual pretende ironicamente significar ao rei, "per razões que pera isso lhe dá a feiticeira, quanto necessários são os feitiços" para conjurarem a felicidade dos próprios fidalgos da sua casa.[28]

While on the topic of witches, let us not forget the necromancer-priest who opened the *Exortação da Guerra* by conjuring up not only devils but also great figures from antiquity who praised and extolled the glory of "famoso Portugal." It is clear that one especial intention of the play is to demonstrate that Portugal's might and valor would have roused the envy of even the superhuman heroes of antiquity; the fantastic element helps to dramatize and accentuate this intention.

Gypsies, a nomadic people known throughout Europe for their

claim to foretell the future by reading one's palm, are the protagonists of the brief *Farsa das Ciganas*. Like the *Auto das Fadas*, the
play portrays the interaction between court members and agents of
the supernatural. Four gypsy youths desire to trade horses with the
noblemen, but are dissuaded by their female companions, who in
turn encourage them to sing and dance. For lucre, the gypsy girls
predict the inevitable fortunes of the ladies of the court, after first
awakening their curiosity by offering to teach them spells for
different desired results. Here are the effects of such spells, which
must have been common knowledge to the Portuguese of the epoch:

> *Luc.* Hechizos sabreiz para que sepaiz
> Los pensamientoz de cuantos miraiz,
> Que dicen, que encumbren, para vuestro avizo.
>
> *Mar.*   Otro hechizo, que pozais mudar
> La voluntad de hombre cualquiera,
> Por firme que esté con fe verdadera,
> Y vuz lo mudeiz á vuestro mandar.
>
> *Gir.*   Otro hechizo os puedo yo dar
> Con que pudaiz, señuraz, saber
> Cual es el marido que habeiz de tener,
> Y el dia y la hora que habeiz de cazar.

(5:322-23)

The fantastic element fulfilled a dual function in the piece: it
offered the audience, much to its delight, a combination of drama
with popular necromancy; it also enabled Gil Vicente to satirize the
niggardliness of the courtiers who (at least in this instance) paid the
gypsies very poorly for their predictions. Observe the satirical note
on which a gypsy girl concludes the presentation: "No vi gente tan
honrada / Dar tan poco galardon."

The tragicomedy *Cortes de Júpiter*, composed for the departure
of the princess Beatriz to marry the Duke of Savoy, is a hodgepodge
of fantastical elements. God sends Providence, attired as a princess,
to Jupiter with the request that he allay the elements so the planned
voyage to Savoy would be favorable. Providence exits and the Four
Winds enter; blowing their trumpets, they summon the Sea, the Sun,
the Moon, and Venus. As if this were not fantastic enough, Thomas
R. Hart professes that from this point on "the rest of the play is a
sort of preview, transferred to the plane of fantasy, of the princess's
sailing, which was to take place after the performance."[29]

Jupiter then proposes that the entire court, all transformed into fish, accompany the fleet on the first leg of the voyage. The Winds summon the planet Mars, which arrives with its signs: Cancer, Leo, and Capricorn. Mars has the Enchanted Mooress Thais brought forth, her enchantment sundered by song. This Enchanted Mooress was directly derived from the Portuguese folk legends, according to Maria A. Zaluar Nunes:

> Gil Vicente também registou a tradição ainda hoje persistente, sobretudo entre o povo do sul do país, de que ha mouras encantadas, guardadoras de tesouros inestimáveis, que esperam pela hora do desencantamento, e reservam, a quem tiver a dita de o conseguir, preciosidades de alta valia: jardins maravilhosos, ouro, pedrarias e objectos mágicos.[30]

Mars announces the extraordinary gifts the Mooress will give the princess to bring her good fortune:

> E a Moura há de trazer
> três cousas que vos disser,
> pera do estreito avante.
> Um anel seu encantado,
> e um didal de condam,
> e o precioso treçado
> que foi no campo tomado
> depois de morto Roldam.
>
> (4:256)

Mars then reveals the practical purpose of these articles:

> O terçado pera vencer;
> o didal é tam facundo,
> que tudo lhe fará trazer;
> o anel pera saber
> o que se faz polo mundo.
>
> (4:256)

The members of the court conclude this fantastical piece in song.

The motive for all this magical pageantry was to pay homage to the Portuguese royal family and to exalt Portuguese accomplishments in their newly acquired territories. Also, there is an ulterior motive that is omnipresent in Vicentine drama: the satire of professions and individuals. This is the function of the fish-transformation episode. In it we find the contemptuous metamorphosis of students into frogs because of their rambunctiousness, of lawyers into sharks because of their insatiability, of the renowned Portuguese poet Garcia de Resende into a drum-fish for his portliness, and of the king's advisor

Gil Vaz da Cunha into a whale for the very same reason.

Mermaids are often mentioned and figure prominently in the *Triunfo do Inverno*. Their appearance comes immediately after the scene of the sea storm and, in a lovely *romance*, they praise—as in all Vicentine courtly presentations—Portugal's past and present.

The *Divisa da Cidade de Coimbra*, a fantastic tale in dramatic form, provides Master Gil's own interpretations of how a princess, a lion, a serpent, and a calyx came to figure in the coat of arms of city of Coimbra. In the drama, Gil Vicente alludes to Ovid's *Metamorphoses* with its humorous version of the origin of Mondego as the river's name and of how the hare came about:

> Monderigon morto, segundo se prova
> fizeram-lhe a cova lá cima num pégo,
> pollo qual se chama este rio Mondego;
> e a sepultura se diz Penacova.
> Fogio Liberata da furia disforme,
> e indo fogindo miu fraca e miu febre,
> tornou-se animal que se chama lebre,
> que de Liberata tomou este nome.
>
> (3:162)

Dragons are also mentioned; however, none ever participates in any play's action. Their role is limited to brief allusions to their wickedness, as this extract from the peasant's plaintive speech to the hermit in the *Divisa da Cidade de Coimbra* illustrates:

> Vino Dios ya sin razon,
> estando resando ella
> en mi corral,
> consentió que un dragon
> me hiciese biudo della,
> por mi mal.
>
> (3:138)

An observation by Maria A. Zaluar Nunes regarding Gil Vicente's frequent use of the fantastic is of interest:

> Também nos parece que a introdução do maravilhoso nas peças de Gil Vicente deve corresponder à necessidade duma momentânea fuga da realidade, do quadro habitual.[31]

This is true of all writers of Menippea; the genre's carnivalized roots demand that the protagonists venture into the realm of the supernatural. Had the Menippea eschewed the illusory, it would not have exerted such influence. Its one-sided realism, along with its mordant satire of mores and social groups, would have made of it just another exposé. It is the blend of comic satire with daring fantasies that best thematically defines the Menippea and its correlative genres.

The representations of man's unusual, abnormal moral and psychic states are characteristic of the Menippea.

The Menippea presents all sorts of psychological and moral abnormalities: many varieties of madness ("maniac themes"), split personalities, constant daydreaming, bizarre dreams and visions, passions bordering on insanity, suicides, etc. These various abnormalities, though not thematic per se, influence the very form of the genre. Dreams, daydreams, and madness negate man's epic-tragic integrity and destiny by revealing another ego within him and evidencing the possibility of an entirely different existence. It is as if man ceases to mean only one thing to, or coincide with, himself and surrenders his uniqueness and sense of direction, just as at a later time Freudian psychology would show the human being as the unwitting subject of often unsuspected unconscious drives.

In the epic, dreams also occur; they are intended to motivate or caution man. They do not take him beyond the limits of his fate and character, nor do they destroy his integrity. In truth, man's schism with himself and his resulting loss of purposeful direction are found only embryonically in the Menippea. Nevertheless, they are included and offer a totally different view of man. The split of man with himself (the schizophrenic personality) is characterized by man's dialogical attitude toward himself, and internal debate between man and his conscience.

The opening lines of the *Auto da Sibila Cassandra* constitute an interior dialogue between Cassandra and her conscience:

> Quien mete ninguno andar
> ni porfiar
> en casamientos comigo!
> pués séame Dios testigo
> que yo digo
> que no me quiero casar.
> Cual será pastor nacido
> tan polido
> ahotas que me meresca!
> alguno hay que me paresca
> en cuerpo, vista y sentido?

> Cual es la dama polida,
> que su vida
> juega, pues pierde casando,
> su libertad cautivando,
> otorgando
> que sea siempre vencida,
> desterrada en mano agena,
> siempre en pena,
> abatida y sojùzgada?
> Y piensan que ser casada
> que es alguna buena estrena!
>
> (1:49-50)

With this initial interior dialogue, the image of the narrator and the tone of the piece are characterized. A girl intent on deviating from the norm is about to get out of the rut that is her life, and will oppose everyone. Her outlook, as revealed later, is shaped by a "crisis dream or vision," which in the Menippea often serves as a genre-setting theme:

> Yo tengo en mi fantasia,
> y juraria
> que de mi ha de nacer [Christ];
> que otra de mi merecer
> no puede haber,
> en bondad ni hidalguia.
>
> (1:70)

It is the theme of rebirth and renewal through a dream or vision that permits one to see in his mind's eye the possibility of a completely different existence on earth. In the epic, this vision did not destroy the unity of the real world and did not create a second plane; nor, as noted above, did it destroy the simple integrity of the hero's image. The epic vision was not counterposed to ordinary life as a possible alternative.

Cassandra's vision, on the other hand, is introduced precisely as such a possibility, a completely different existence organized in accordance with laws other than those of earthly life. The life seen in her vision makes her actual existence seem unnatural, forcing a reevaluation of her reality. Cassandra is now at odds with her milieu. Thus, her vision creates an incompatibility with ordinary life that serves one of the goals of the Menippea: to test the idea and the possessor of the idea.

Immediately after Cassandra's presumptuous revelation to Abraham, Isaiah, and Solomon, her "uncles" in the play, she becomes the object of the following commentaries:

> *Abr.*   Ya Casandra desvaria.
> *Esa.*   Yo diria
>   que está muy cerca de loca,
>   y su cordura es muy poca,
>   pues que toca
>   tan alta descortesia.
> *Sal.*   . . . .
>   Casandra, segun que muestra
>   esa respuesta
>   tan fuera de conclusion,
>   tu loca, yo Salomon,
>   dame razon,
>   qué vida fuera la nuestra?
>
>   (1:70)

What has been thought all along, but unstated, is now expressed: Cassandra is insane. However, her insanity, or more properly, her delusion is temporary in nature, as her eventual enlightenment before Christ's manger demonstrates.

A fine illustration of a disturbed emotional state bordering on suicide is Rubena's soliloquy (a dialogical attitude toward herself) in the opening scene of the *Comédia de Rubena*. Alone and stricken with labor pains, Rubena laments her situation in a dialogue between herself and her conscience:

>   Oh, triste de mí Rubena!
> á quien me descubriré?
> á quien contaré mi pena?
> como porné en mano agena
> mi vida, mi honra y fé?
> Oh mocedad desdichada,
> de falso amor engañada,
> engañada sin sentido!
> qué haré desemparada?
> qué haré triste preñada
> sin marido?
>
>   (3:5)

Her self-interrogation continues until, despairing, she longs for death:

> Quien tuviera, ó quien hallara
> una preciosa vara,
> que tuviera tal condon,

que improviso me llevara
a alguno que me sacara
el corazon?

. . . .

Duélanvos mis tristes hadas,
y llevadme apresuradas
áquel valle de tristura,
donde estan las mal hadadas,
donde estan las sin ventura
sepultadas.

. . . .

Yo misma quiero el morir.

(3:5-6)

She confides in her maid Benita and keeps mentioning her forthcoming demise, which by this point she believes will happen in childbirth. Were this a tragedy, the death wish would inevitably be fulfilled, since Rubena's impregnation by a priest and her resulting mental state violate the stringent codes of the genre. Tragedy's finality in its plots is inalterable. Yet, in the Menippea and related genres, finality is abolished and man is permitted to alter his situation so as to avoid the seemingly inevitable. Subsequently, the conjured devils transport Rubena to a mountain top and the narrator explains:

Llevaron nel aire ansí á Rubena
aquellos espritos á una montaña:
parió una hija, mas linda de España,
segun trataremos en estotra cena.
Como se vido ya fuera de pena,
echó sus vestidos en una ribera,
ceñió su camisa las carnes de fuera,
hermosa en cabello como una sirena.

(3:25)

Once she is out of danger thanks to the supernatural forces in the comedy, Rubena's state of depression is shed along with her clothes, and an entirely new life opens to her.

Since the flexibility of the serio-comic genres obviates dogmatic predictability, the third scene of the same playlet contains a somewhat analogous situation, but with an altogether different conclusion: Felicio decides to withdraw to a desolate area and await his end after his rejection by Cismena, Rubena's child, who orders him to leave her sight forever. There he enters into a dialogue with his echo—in a way, an extension of his conscience. Working himself into a frenzy, he repeats several times his wish to die. Unlike the case of Rubena, however, the tragic integrity and finality are not shattered by his altered psychic state: he perishes (a tragic ending).

The very nature of drama makes it difficult to introduce a character with a split personality. The brevity demanded by the need to keep the audience's attention militates against extended exposition of any character's psyche. Nevertheless, sometimes the plot may require unusual behavior by the protagonist in order to advance the action. Only in this manner can we explain the savage Monderigon's bizarre behavior in the *Divisa da Cidade de Coimbra*. In the presence of Liberata, he is meek and polite:

> Digo que yo me ire, señora:
> hecho está.
> Mandadme vos, rosa mia,
> que este siervo hará luego
> tu mandado.
>
> (3:151)

When he returns later, his tone changes completely upon finding Celiponcio, Liberata's brother, in her company. He draws his weapon and says menacingly:

> Confiésate, hombre cuitado,
> que no quiero que mas vivas.
> . . . .
> Hace tú con tu hermana,
> que me quiera bien no mas,
> y que se vaya comigo.
>
> (3:161)

Monderigon's sudden changes in temperament could certainly be attributed to his burning passion for Liberata; however, the plot itself demands these radical alterations so that its action can take place within theatrical time limitations. What seems inconsistent behavior on Monderigon's part is primarily a plot device to assure that the object of the play—the explanation of the elements on Coimbra's coat of arms—is successfully effected in dramatic fashion.

Farsa do Velho da Horta offers a radical psychological change in the play's main character, the Old Man. Happily married and advanced in years, he enters his orchard to amuse himself. Laying eyes on a young girl who has come to gather greens, he suddenly falls in love. Segismundo Spina views this sudden change as a comic device:

O cômico tem como fonte uma série de inadaptações, desde o início da farsa: a mudança psicológica inesperada no espírito do Velho que, espairecendo, calmo, pela horta é acometido por uma paixão repentina, à primeira vista e de efeitos fulminantes.[32]

The Menippea gives rise to new artistic categories of the scandalous and the eccentric.

Bakhtin points out that the Menippea is characterized by all sorts of scandalous scenes, eccentric behavior, incongruous speeches and performances—in short, by a predilection for violation of the commonly accepted (the ordinary course of events) and that which is considered within behavioral norms, as well as verbal propriety. The artistic structure of these scandalous scenes sets them far apart from epic heroics and tragic catastrophes. In the Menippea, it may be said, emerge new artistic categories of the scandalous and the eccentric incompatible with the classical epic and tragedy. Scandals and eccentricities rend the epic and tragic integrity of the world, sundering the proper, dignified order of human activities and interaction and liberating behavior from predetermined norms and motivations. The "incongruous word or speech," either through its cynical candor, since it profanes the sacrosanct, or through its crude trespass upon etiquette, abounds in the Menippea.

This characteristic was common in late medieval literature, and Vicentine drama is no exception. The scandalous and eccentric were included to create a free and light play dealing with archetypes and concepts, but there was another, more remote and prophetic goal: to dispel the atmosphere of gloom and official gravity that permeated society, to change its demeanor, to render it more human, closer to man and his nature, more intelligible and easier to bear.

In other words, the scandalous and eccentric episodes in many late medieval works, far from the isolated commonplace obscenity of modern times, are organic parts of a large and complex world of popular marketplace forms. Only when separated from their origin and seen under a modern light do such situations appear in poor taste. The use of the "inappropriate" was for Gil Vicente a means justified by its end, not an end in itself.

The farce *Quem Tem Farelos?*, presented in 1515—the *Copilaçam* erroneously records 1505—opens with two servants, Apariço and Ordonho, seeking bran for their masters' mounts. Each voices his complaints about the privation he endures at his master's home. Aires Rosado, a boastful and conceited squire who is Apariço's master, spends his entire day writing poetry and playing his guitar because he is in love. With night drawing near, he decides to serenade his beloved Isabel. As soon as he starts to sing, the neighborhood dogs begin to bark. Meanwhile, his servant makes acerbic commentaries about him. Isabel appears at the window, but what she says must be deduced from Aires Rosado's responses. His vainglorious boasts are accompanied by a veritable animal chorus —dogs barking, cats meowing, a rooster crowing—as well as by the comical observations of his servant. The girl's mother emerges and attempts to put an end to the amorous dialogue by heaping invective on the squire. Nonetheless, he ignores her and continues singing his verses. When Aires Rosado finally departs, mother and daughter argue about propriety:

> Vel.　　Que dirá a vizinhança?
> 　　　　Dize, má mulher sem siso!
> Isa.　　Que tenho eu de ver co'isso.
> Vel.　　Como tens tão má criança!
> Isa.　　Algum demo valho eu,
> 　　　　e algum demo mereço,
> 　　　　e algum demo pareço,
>
> 　　　　pois que cantam polo meu.
> 　　　　　Vós quereis que me despeje,
> 　　　　vós quereis que tenha modos,
> 　　　　que pareça bem a todos
> 　　　　e ninguem não me deseje?
>
> 　　　　　　　　　　　　　　　(5:84)

Isabel protests that weaving and sewing are not for her and states her preference for the niceties of courtship. She embodies the typical nubile maiden of that period who thought only about money and status.

The mother's preoccupation with what the neighbors would say about Isabel's nocturnal rendezvous (a scandal) seems incongruous with the scandal she herself surely created by cursing the squire; yet, it must be stressed that the scandal was not the result of her vulgar language but of the disturbance created by her shouts in the late hours of the night. Curses and obscenities were used during Master Gil's time to elicit laughter (this type of language was associated with lower-class speech, a level of discourse that court members found amusing) and not for their shock value. Óscar de Pratt corroborates this view:

O requinte de polidez palaciana, que atingiu o mais alto coeficiente na época manuelina, tinha o valor relativo ao grau das convenções sociais do tempo. Os trovadores do *Cancioneiro* punham freqüentemente a nu,

em despejadas trovas de maldizer—causa de formidáveis troças 'e, por vezes, de rixas sangrentas—, certos casos equívocos da vida do paço, em que grosseiramente atingiam as próprias damas da rainha com a sátira mordente das alusões obscenas.
Neste meio, em que certas liberdades sociais, que hoje se nos antolham inconvenientes, tinham compreesão diversa, não hesitaria decerto Gil Vicente em fazer representar o seu inocente esboço de crítica social. Em 1509 já ele tinha feito representar, *à mui católica rainha D. Leonor,* essa peça de arrojada concepção realista que intitulou *Auto da Índia.*[33]

Besides its purpose to amuse, the scandalous, billingsgate-laden scene has another aim: to convey the message that young people from humble surroundings detested their condition and dreamed of a better future. Isabel's words bespeak her desire for a way of life not in keeping with her lowly station in society:

> Ir a miúde ao espelho,
> e poer de branco e vermelho,
> e outras cousas que eu sei:
> pentear, curar de mim
> e poer a ceja em dereito;
> e morder por meu proveito
> estes beicinhos assi.

(5:86)

This statement is contradictory from a sixteenth-century aristocratic audience's viewpoint. Isabel, by expressing these concerns and ignoring those appropriate for a "wench" like her, has transgressed the normal logic of life. Her eccentric behavior has put her at odds with herself and her surroundings. But, after all, are real human beings not conflictive and more often than not at odds with themselves?

A humanist, Master Gil understood only too well that, if drama was to convey any social message while remaining entertaining, it had to be made more human, more accessible, more easily identifiable with man's idiosyncrasies and eccentricities, i.e., more psychological. Isabel's revolt against her ascribed and "predetermined" status was not at all surprising in a sixteenth-century Portugal rocked by rapid social change: man was starting to look more to himself for decisions affecting his life rather than to the rigid feudal structure that for centuries had controlled his existence.

Such was the case with the Mofina Mendes and Inês Pereira in the works bearing their respective names. Both sought a better life and both exhibited scandalous and eccentric behavior. The Mofina

Mendes neglects the herd with which she has been entrusted, while Inês chooses to marry outside her class, to everyone's displeasure. Unlike Isabel's case, where we do not know the outcome of her rebellious stance, in these two instances we are given the results: the Mofina Mendes, after receiving a jug of olive oil in payment for her botched job as a shepherdess, accidentally drops it; Inês Pereira ends up marrying a boor after her scoundrel husband, whom she wed for his musical talents amid much controversy, was killed fighting the Muslims.

In each of these plays, eccentric or scandalous behavior is subordinated to the axiom the author wishes to exemplify: in the *Auto da Mofina Mendes*, he was trying to convey that human delights, like the jug of oil, will crash to the ground and come to an end; in the *Farsa de Inês Pereira* the message is that "it is better to have a donkey that will carry you than a horse that will throw you." These thematic axioms justify the Mofina's eccentric indifference before her bad luck, and Inês's controversial decision to marry the squire and her later scandalous cuckolding of her new husband.

A fine example of an incongruous speech appears in the opening lines of the *Auto da Índia*, part of a dialogue between the main personage Constança (*ama*) and her servant girl (*moça*):

> *Moç.* Jesu! Jesu! que é ora isso?
> É porque se parte a armada?
> *Ama* Olhade a mal estreada!
> Eu hei-de chorar por isso?
> *Moç.* Por minha'alma, que cuidei
> e que sempre imaginei
> que choráveis por noss'amo.
> *Ama* Por qual demo ou por qual gamo
> ali má hora chorarei?
> Como me leixa saudosa!
> Toda eu fico amargurada!
> *Moç.* Pois porque estais anojada?
> Dizei-m'o por vida vossa.
> *Ama* Leixai-me ora eramá,
> que dizem que não vai já.
>
> (5:89-90)

Constança's lamentations clearly run counter to the joy expected from a wife whose husband may be spared a long absence. Her consternation over her husband's possible stay and the incongruousness of her personality throughout the play have the character of hysteria; she possesses no naive integrity. She is a madwoman. Her insanity and the scandalous infidelities resulting from this condition create a situation that breaks with what is "seemly," that which society considers proper for a married woman.

Yet, the *Auto da Índia*, in keeping with the nature of the genre, is not an exposé of the different moral behavior brought about by the voyages to India. Constança's infidelities antecede her husband's departure, as she herself admits:

> Hi se vai ele a pescar
> meia légua polo mar,
> isto bem o sabes tu;
> quanto mais a Calecu:
> quem ha tanto d'esperar?

(5:93)

These examples, chosen to illustrate this characteristic, do not exhaust those to be found in the extant forty-four pieces. Others could also be cited: the scandalous encounter between the Old Man and his wife in *Farsa do Velho da Horta*, or some of the earthy exchanges between the Devil and certain departing souls in the *Trilogia das Barcas*.

The Menippea contains many sharp contrasts and oxymoronic combinations.

Bakhtin states that the Menippea contains many sharp contrasts and oxymoronic combinations: the virtuous prostitute, the true freedom of a sage though he be a slave by status, the noble thief, the wealthy man who becomes a slave to his passions, moral downfall and purification, luxury and squalor, etc. The Menippea shows a preference for sharp transitions and alterations, ups and downs, unexpected comings together of distant and different things—in short, *mésalliances* of all types. It is through this characteristic and the previous one, as Suzana Camargo notes, that one obtains a clear picture of what Bakhtin calls "carnivalization," the effect of carnival on literature. Both characteristics arise from the aforementioned four categories inherent in a carnivalesque perception of the world: eccentricity, familiarity, *mésalliances*, and profanation.[34]

This characteristic is common to the majority of Gil Vicente's playlets. Often we find the rustic rubbing elbows with the courtier (*Clérigo da Beira*), the secular interwoven with the religious (*Floresta de Enganos*), the pagan employed to substantiate Christian doctrine (*Auto da Feira*). These united antinomies stem directly from carni-

val's two-in-one images, which combine within themselves the anti-
podes of change and crisis: birth and death (the image of pregnant
death), benediction and damnation (the benedictory carnival curses,
with simultaneous wishes of death and rebirth), praise and condem-
nation, youth and old age, top and bottom, face and backside,
stupidity and wisdom.

In the *Comédia do Viúvo*, Prince Rosvel not only undergoes a
sudden physical transformation by disguising himself as an ignorant
laborer, but is also able to make the linguistic transition that his new
role demands:

> Nada, nada, jurí á san:
> venía yo haciendo
> tu ru ru ru ru,
> viene el hideputa can,
> que lo yo encomiendo.
>
> (3:104)

He embodies the oxymoronic combination lord/commoner, making
possible what in ordinary life would have been unlikely: the eventual
marriage of a nobleman to a merchant's daughter. In the manner of
the Menippea, the piece presents us with the unusual union of two
individuals who, though not social peers, are joined through the
genre's total freedom of invention. In the epitome of such freedom,
Rosvel's brother, Dom Gilberto, unexpectedly arrives in *deus ex
machina* fashion to wed the merchant's other daughter whom Rosvel
had courted simultaneously. Later, in Spanish Golden Age drama,
this type of "poetic justice" as ending would enjoy great popularity
among playwrights.

Again in the *Divisa da Cidade de Coimbra*, characters take on
carnival overtones and form two-in-one images. A farmer appears
bemoaning his fate in the *serra*. A hermit arrives and asks him the
causes of his problems. The farmer explains:

> Yo soy hombre generoso
> de noble sangre nacido,
> y por huir
> del estado peligroso,
> mudé, por no ser perdido,
> mi vivir,
> escogiendo por mejor,
> para el ánima salvar
> de afrenta
> la vida del labrador,
> que no tiene de que dar

tanta cuenta.

              (3:137)

 The desire to escape his noble lineage by choosing the life of a farmer is in keeping with the structure of a two-in-one image. Bakhtin defines this structure as one that strives to encompass and unite within itself both poles of evolution or both halves of an antithesis. The upper pole of a two-in-one image is reflected in the lower, in the manner of figures on playing cards. The prince opted for a way of life dramatically opposed to his own because opposites, since they are reflected in one another, know and understand each other. It then seems not at all bizarre that the hermit too is of royal stock:

> Yo soy el Rei Ceridon
> de Cordoba y Andalusía;
> y un salvage,
> á que llaman Monderigon
> cativó una hija mia,
> por mi ultrage.

              (3:144)

Until this point, Master Gil has presented two individuals who unite in their *personae* the contradictory roles of lord/commoner. With the declaration by Ceridon that his daughter has been abducted by the savage Monderigon, the existing contrasts shift from an oxymoronic combination in the self to the thematic *mésalliance* of beauty and the beast. However, it is not with this abduction that the beauty/beast *mésalliance* is elaborated—Monderigon and Colimena (the king's daughter) never meet on stage—but in the scene where Monderigon meets Liberata, the farmer's daughter.

 Hearing her singing in the woods, Monderigon approaches Liberata; frightened by the savage's appearance, she calls out to her brother. Monderigon, beholding the maiden's beauty, falls madly in love with her. The savage's personality undergoes an immediate and radical change. He ceases to be cruel and becomes most gentle:

> Digo que yo me ire, señora:
> hecho está.
> Mandadme vos, rosa mia,
> que este siervo hará luego
> tu mandado.

              (3:151)

Already in this scene, within a brief period of time, two sharp contrasts have emerged: the beauty with the beast and the gentle savage. Monderigon departs at Liberata's request and, finding herself alone, she declaims:

> Es ido: pues por mi fé
> que no sé por qué interese
> deseaba que se fuese,
> y pésame porque se fue,
> como si bien le quisiese.
> . . . .
> Por ventura es enemigo,
> que quiere hacerme herege:
> mas no rege,
> que el amor sento comigo.
>
> (3:152)

The ambivalent feeling (love/disdain) expressed in this soliloquy exemplifies the very nature of human emotions. In this world everything lives hard by its opposite. Love lives on the very border of disdain, which it knows and understands, and disdain lives on the border of love, which it also knows and understands. Constança's— the name itself, given her adulterous ways, an ironic underscoring of this ambivalence—feelings toward her husband, in the *Auto da Índia*, and, to a certain degree, Inês's relationship with Pero Marques in the *Farsa de Inês Pereira* are of this same type.

On certain occasions, the frequently employed nobleman/rustic *mésalliance* takes on such familiarity that hierarchical barriers are broken and profanation, a carnival category, invades the conversation. In the *Auto dos Reis Magos*, a knight, accompanied by the Magi, has lost his way to Bethlehem and, coming upon two rustics and a hermit, asks in a friendly manner to be set on the right path. After receiving an impudent answer from Valerio, one of the rustics, the knight engages him in the following exchange of insults:

> *Cav.*   Mira bien, pastor, que dices.
> *Val.*   En frente de las narices
> a perdices
> andarás, prometo á mí.
> *Cav.*   Qué linage tan bestial!
> animal
> este bruto pastoriego!
> *Val.*   Doy á rabia el palaciego,
> por san pego
> que quizás por vuestro mal...

(1:43-44)

As in carnival, these individuals, though social opposites, meet on an
equal plane to abuse one another verbally. Whereas in carnival itself
this type of freedom would have been the result of carnival's anti-
hierarchical nature, in this piece it is brought about by the knight's
initial menacing warning; it lowered his status to that of the rustic by
giving the latter the hope of possibly facing him, a knight, in combat.

Antithetic couplings are also found in the expositions made by
certain characters. After the Angel announces the birth of Christ in
the *Auto Pastoril Castelhano*, the shepherd Gil Terron astonishes his
companions with his knowledge of the Scriptures. Among the many
things he divulges concerning Christ's birth, this next description of
the newly born is of special interest for its contrasting adjectives:

> Aquel niño es eternal,
> invisible y visible;
> es mortal y immortal,
> mobible y immobible,

(1:30)

In Christ, as in carnival, these contradictions are inseparable, they
are two-in-one, and they transmute into one another; if they are
separated, their doctrinal significance—or therapeutic significance,
vis-à-vis carnival—is completely lost. Christ, like carnival, must
embody the extraordinary, the contradictory, that which contravenes
the normal course of events.

As observed, the ineffable human emotion known as love is
contradictory. It not only lives on the border of its very opposite,
hatred, but also encompasses a panoply of inner conflicts. Colopen-
dio, a victim of love in the *Romagem de Agravados*, expresses the
contradictory nature of love in his querulous entrance speech:

> Quando falo, estou calado;
> quando estou, entonces ando;
> quando ando, estou quedado;
> quando durmo, estou acordado;
> quando acordo, estou sonhando;
> quando chamo, então respondo;
> quando choro, entonces rio;
> quando me queimo, hei frio;
> quando me mostro, m'escondo;
> quando espero, desconfio.

(5:12)

Thus far, we have commented on various oxymoronic combinations in Vicentine drama. To a certain degree, these have been readily apparent to the spectator or reader. There are, however, contrasting pairs that are perceived not by the senses but by the intellect. We refer to the symbolical contrasts inserted in various plays, especially the allegorical ones. With regard to such contrasts, António J. Saraiva and Óscar Lopes offer this point of view:

> Nos autos alegóricos religiosos, o real quotidiano exerce uma função muito definida: faz sobressair, pelo contraste, o carácter absoluto, imutável, permanente do sobrenatural. É neles flagrante a busca de um efeito de oposição entre os dois mundos que lembra os pintores que, como o seu contemporâneo Fr. Carlos, contrapõem a transparência luminosa das figuras sagradas a espessura opaca das personagens terrestres.
>
> No *Auto dos Mistérios da Virgem*, mais conhecido pelo nome de *Mofina Mendes*, patenteia-se este efeito de contraste entre o profano e o divino, entre as trevas e a luz. O *intermezzo* pastoril que deu o nome ao auto exerce uma função dentro do simbolismo real da peça, materializado e resumido no pote de azeite que a Mofina, bailando, deixa cair no chão. Acentua, por contraste, a interpolaridade do mundo ideal, representado pela Virgem, pelas personificações das virtudes e pelos anjos, cuja linguagem reveste uma solenidade litúrgica, realçada pelo latim das Escrituras. A própria Mofina é ambígua (ora pastora real, ora personificação da sorte mofina), e o dramaturgo, num rasgo, salta finalmente da sua risível leviandade individual à consciência amarga de que, afinal, todos temos o nosso pote de azeite "que há dar consigo em terra."[35]

The Menippea includes elements of social utopia.

In the Menippea, elements of social utopia are introduced in the form of dreams and journeys to unknown lands. According to Bakhtin, the utopian element combines organically with all the other elements of the genre.

The *Trilogia das Barcas*, in which souls journey to their eternal destination, could be seen in light of a social utopia. This applies to the first two parts—the *Barca do Inferno* and the *Barca do Purgatório* —for it is here that justice is done irrespective of social position and that individuals, if meritorious, end up in an everlasting utopian society: Heaven. Those assigned to purge their sins along the shore (Purgatory) share the hope that, once God deems it fitting, they too will be transported to the Heaven of the opposite shore and join the fortunate ones. Those remaining, the truly unredeemable, must embark on the Hell-bound ship.

Yet, the mere point of departure, because of the impartial

decisions made there, creates a utopian atmosphere. Those who are damned include: a nobleman, a usurer, a cobbler, a friar, a panderess, a Jew, a judge, a public prosecutor, a hanged man, and a gambler. Those who must do penance on Purgatory's shore are a farmer, a market-woman, a shepherd, and a shepherdess. The others, who gain the Kingdom of Heaven include a fool, four knights, and a young child. Notice the debasing tone of the devil's words in his dialogue with the judge:

> *Cor.* E onde vai o batel?
> *Dia.* No Inferno vos poremos.
> *Cor.* Como! à terra dos Demos
> há de ir um Corregedor?
> *Dia.* Santo descorregedor,
> embarcai e remaremos.
> Ora entrai, pois que viestes.
> *Cor.* *Non est de regula juris,* não.
> *Dia.* *Ita, ita,* dai cá a mão,
> remareis um remo destes.
> Fazei conta que nascestes
> pera nosso companheiro.
>
> (2:70)

The devil's retorts "discrown" the judge, presenting him with a career alternative befitting his impending fate: an oarsman, a simple manual laborer. This is not to say that lower-class people had a greater propensity to sin, but that, of all people, a judge should not have led such an unprincipled life.

In the *Barca da Glória*, Master Gil was compelled by circumstance to save the "persons of truly high rank" with whom the play deals. A count, a duke, a king, an emperor, a bishop, an archbishop, and a pope parade before the devil. Horrified at the possibility of going to Hell, these sinners begin to pray and appeal to the angel, attesting to their faith and love of God; but the angel is unable to help and suggests they entrust themselves to the Almighty. Seeing the ship of Heaven about to leave without them, these important figures start to weep and to show their contrition. Suddenly God, who has been listening to them, appears as Christ resurrected and carries them off with him.

One of the principal factors that forced the dramatist's hand was his complete dependency on the members of the court. The plays were written for and presented at court and, consequently, Master Gil had no option but to spare those characters who symbolized his benefactors. For these, notwithstanding their peccadillos, there had to be a spot in the utopia known as Heaven—Gil Vicente is here playing politics, a necessary thing if he was to get his plays produced. Surely, had he been self-supporting, no social group would have received preferential treatment. As it was, it was quite daring on his part to suggest that these figures were damned and gained salvation only through God's direct intervention.

The *Auto da Fama* an allegory of Portugal's maritime discoveries and exploits, contains what may well be a utopian vision: the spiritual unity of the two Peninsular countries. A Portuguese woman named Fama (Fame), aided by the fool Joane, is a duckkeeper in the province of Beira. She is wooed by a Frenchman, an Italian, and a Castilian but remains indifferent to their overtures. She demands that each of them listen while she recounts the glories of Portugal. In the conversation with the Castilian, Fame makes this comment concerning her neighboring country:

> Pois Marrocos,
> que sempre fez dez mil biocos
> até destruir Espanha,
> sabei se se tornou aranha,
> quando viu o demo em socos.
> Bem: e é rezão que me vá
> donde há cousas tão honradas
> tão devotas, tão soadas?
> O lavor vos contará.
> I-vos embora.
>
> (5:136-37)

The Castilian realizes the truth of her remarks and replies:

> Quedáos á Dios, señora;
> no quiero mas porfias.
>
> (5:137)

Subsequently, the Castilian comes upon the Frenchman and the Italian. The three comment on what Fame has said. The Frenchman and the Italian recognize that her struggle against the enemies of Christianity is a most worthy cause and, with this realization, the Castilian confesses:

> Por eso no porfié
> con ella, ni es razon,
> porque sus victorias son
> muy lejos y por la fé.
>
> (5:138-39)

With these words the Castilian may be verbalizing Gil Vicente's hope that Spain and Portugal, although geographically divided, may unite under the great Catholic mission of warring on the infidel. About this possible utopian vision, F. E. de Tejada Spinola states:

A fama, donzela lusitana, esclarece que os merecimentos do povo vizinho, ganhos ao defender a Espanha dos ataques de "Marrocos", justificam a nacionalidade que ela escolheu e o castelhano é o primeiro a elogiar esses merecimentos e a desejar a continuação de tais triunfos que não inveja, segundo a sua própria declaração, porque são mais do que vitórias exclusivamente portuguesas, são vitórias de toda Espanha, triunfos de um povo hispânico em defesa da cristandade.[36]

The dramatist's desire for a harmonious social order underlies the creation of *Triunfo do Inverno*. Gil Vicente opens the play himself, employing the common classical poetic theme of *ubi sunt*; he contrasts the present sadness in Portugal to the merriment of years past:

> Em Portugal ví eu ja
> em cada casa pandeiro,
> e gaita em cada palheiro;
> e de vinte anos a ca
> não ha hi gaita nem gaiteiro.
> A cada porta um terreiro,
> cada aldea dez folias,
> cada casa atabaqueiro;
> e agora Jeremias
> he nosso tamborileiro.
>
> (4:261-62)

He goes on to lament that people no longer sing and dance gaily, but rather sing sad songs.

The sharp contrast between life prior to the twenty-year period cited by the author and the current state of affairs seems to underscore Gil Vicente's desire to return to an era that he considered ideal; Portugal's past happiness, a result of the nation's socio-political stability and harmony, is counterposed to the gloom that marked the last years of D. Manuel and the rise to the throne of the fanatical D. João III. The ensuing verses illustrate the author's yearning for a return to the utopia of yesteryear:

> Se neste tempo de gloria
> nacêra a infanta sagrada,
> como fôra festejada,

sómente polla vitoria
da Rainha alumiada!
Ja tudo leixam passar,
tudo leixam por fazer,
sem pessoa preguntar
a este mesmo pesar
que foi daquele prazer.

(4:264)

The author then declares that he has written a tragicomedy to
fête the birth of this princess, D. Isabel. The figure of Winter appears and boasts about his power. Two shepherds, Brisco and Juan,
curse winter in the mountains. Juan complains that he has spent all
his money on a maiden and, heedless of winter, now cannot afford
garments appropriate for the season. An old woman in love with a
young man also complains of the rigors of winter. After her departure, Winter urges the shepherds to seek shelter because he wants to
stage his second triumph: the unleashing of his fury on a ship that,
if not for a simple sailor who relieves the pilot of his duties, would
have foundered.

The above scenes perhaps incorporate the main utopian outlook
of the entire piece: man must accept his role in the divine scheme of
creation in order to assure social harmony. Both Juan and the old
woman are in a woeful state not because nature has so decreed, but
because their emotions have made them oblivious to reality. The
ship runs into peril less because of the tempest than because the
captain's selfishness has led him to choose an unqualified crew.
Thomas R. Hart's observations are valuable comments on the
episode:

Though the blame for the ship's desperate situation is clearly placed on
the captain, and thus ultimately on the men at court who obtained his
post for him, Vicente obviously sees no inconsistency in inserting an
attack on corruption at court in a play which, like court plays in other
countries, is largely given over to praise of the sovereigns. The reason
is surely that he sees the hope of reforming society not in institutional
reforms but in persuading individual men and women to act differently.
He does not think of creating new social institutions, nor even of
transforming old ones, but rather of returning to the spirit of the
established forms, in the firm conviction that, if only everyone will accept
the obligation of his place in society, things will surely run smoothly once
more.[37]

It was this optimism, this desire for a perfect social order that
combined organically with all other elements of the Menippea and

provided its revitalizing force. Like other writers of Menippea, Gil Vicente's purely carnival faith in the unity of mankind's aspirations and in the goodness of human nature is quite evident in his work.

The Menippea incorporates a mixture of genres.

The Menippea, as Bakhtin points out, characteristically makes wide use of other genres, intercalating such dissimilar genres as the novella, the epistle, the oration, the symposium, etc. It is also characterized by a mixture of prose and verse diction. All intercalated genres are presented with various degrees of parody and objectivization according to the author's varying distances from the author's philosophical position. The verse passages are almost always inserted as parodic humor.

The metric structure of Vicente's drama admits no significant mixture of prose and verse as found in the prosaic Menippeas. There are however instances in which prose does appear intercalated in the corpus of a playlet. One example is the prose narration that follows the scene between the philosopher and the fool in the *Floresta de Enganos*. It is a summary of the action to follow and, although the narrator is not indicated, it may be conjectured that some sort of speaker, similar to the old Greek chorus, recited the lines either onstage or somewhere in the wings.

In the *Auto da Cananeia*, the Lord's Prayer is introduced in Latin so that it may be paraphrased by Christ:

Pater noster qui es in coelis, santificetur nomen tuum adveniat regnum tuum, fiat voluntas tua, sicut in caelo et in terra.

> Com almas limpas e puras
> direis isto ao Senhor,
> firmando-o por criador
> e padre das criaturas,
> que é no Céu emperador.
> E direis com grande amor:
> seja louvado
> teu nome, e santificado
> neste nosso orbe menor
> como és no Céu adorado.

(2:246-47)

Christ is interrupted in his paraphrase by the arrival of the Canaanite woman who, just as did a shepherdess at the outset of the play, alternately sings and speaks in verse:

Canta:

Senhor, filho de Davi,
amerceia-te de mi!
Senhor, filho de Davi,
amerceia-te de mi!

Falado:

Que minha filha é tentada
de espritos que não têm cabo
e minha casa assombrada,
minha câmara pintada,
de figuras do Diabo.

(2:248-49)

The insertion of popular and religious songs in the corpus of the pieces is the most salient structural feature of Vicente's creations, a fact that makes him one of the greatest lyric poets of his time as well as, arguably, its greatest dramatist. Among his inserted spontaneous and simple folkloric lyrics are characteristics inherited directly from the old *Cancioneiros*. There are also traces of *serranilhas* (mountain girl's songs) like this one from the *Farsa dos Almocreves*:

A serra é alta, fria e nevosa,
vi venir serrana, gentil, graciosa.
. . . .
A serra é alta, fria e nevosa,
vi venir serrana, gentil, graciosa.
. . . .
 Vi venir serrana, gentil, graciosa,
cheguei-me per'ela com grã cortesia.
. . . .
 Cheguei-me a ela de grã cortesia,
disse-lhe: Senhora, quereis companhia?
. . . .
 Disse-lhe, senhora, quereis companhia?
Disse-me, Escudeiro, segui vossa via.

(5:349-57)

There are songs evincing similarities to the parallelistic structure of many *cantigas de amigo* (songs in which a maiden voices her emotions toward her absent lover), such as this one in the *Auto da Feira*:

Blanca estais colorada,

Virgem sagrada.
Em Belem villa do amor
da rosa nasceu a flor:
[Blanca estais colorada,]
Virgem sagrada.

Em Belem villa do amor
nasceu a rosa do rosal:
[Blanca estais colorada,]
Virgem sagrada.

(1:245)

The *barcarola* (barcarole) is echoed in this romance sung by three angels who open the *Barca do Purgatório*:

Remando vão remadores
barca de grande alegria;
o patrão que a guiava,
Filho de Deus se dizia.
Anjos eram os remeiros,
que remavam à porfia;
estandarte d'esperança
oh quão bem que parecia!
O mastro da fortaleza
como cristal reluzia;
a vela com fé cosida
todo o mundo esclarecia;
a ribeira mui serena,
que nenhum vento bulia.

(2:83-84)

Cantigas (lays) and *vilancetes* (Spanish *villancicos*) are common insertions, as this *vilancete* from the *Auto da História de Deus* illustrates:

Adorai, montanhas,
o Deus das alturas,
também as verduras;
adorai desertos
e serras floridas,
o Deus dos secretos,
o Senhor das vidas:
ribeiras crecidas,
louvai nas alturas
Deus das criaturas.

(2:185)

There is even an enchanting *zéjel* (a lyric invention of Hispano-Arabic poetry) in the *Auto da Sibila Cassandra* that adheres to its traditional rhyme scheme (aa/bbba/aa/ccca/aa):

> Dicen que me case yo;
> no quiero marido, no.
>
> Mas quiero vivir segura
> nesta sierra á mi soltura,
> que no estar en ventura
> si casaré bien ó no.
>
> Dicen que me case yo;
> no quiero marido, no.
>
> Madre, no seré casada,
> por no ver vida cansada,
> ó quizá mal empleada
> la gracia que Dios me dió.
> Dicen que me case yo;
> no quiero marido, no.
>
> No será ni es nacido
> tal para ser mi marido;
> y pues que tengo sabido
> que la flor yo me la só,
> dicen que me case yo,
> no quiero marido, no.
>
> (1:57-58)

The lullaby sung by the Sorceress to the newly born Cismena in the *Comédia de Rubena* constitutes evidence that mention of the lower bodily parts did not convey the obscene and degrading significance of modern times:

> Ru, ru, menina, ru, ru,
> mouram as velhas e fiques tu
> c'o a tranca no cu.
>
> (3:32)

Had a "tranca no cu" been considered vulgar or offensive, it would not have appeared in the lyrics of a lullaby; its exact meaning, however, is unclear here.

On certain occasions, popular lyrics were included in a composition to meet certain designs of ridicule. Take, for example, the scene in the farce *Quem Tem Farelos?* where the squire Aires Rosado reads aloud *cantigas* in the *Cancioneiro* style which he has turned out for his lady love:

> *Cantiga d'Aires Rosado*
> *a sua Dama,*
> *e não diz como se chama,*
> *de discreto namorado.*
>
> Senhora, pois me lembrais,
> não sejais desconhecida,
> e dai ó demo esta vida
> que me dais.
> . . . .
>
> *Outra sua.*
>
> Pois amor me quer matar
> com dor, tristura e cuidado,

(5:66-67)

The picture is that of a penniless Aires Rosado moving about his squalid abode reciting verses that in both content and structure are ludicrously troubadouresque. What makes the scene even more outlandish is the fact that these *cantigas* are not directed at some noble lady but at a simple "wench."

Master Gil was also fond of parodying religious genres, not to mock or discredit Christian precepts, but because, as a humanist, he had come to resent the mechanical attitude the clergy had developed toward their priestly duties, e.g., prayers, sermons, and masses. This resentment is mirrored in the following parody of a Hail Mary by the black thief of the *Clérigo da Beira* (note that the garbled prayer appears in prose):

Sabe a regina Matho misercoroda nutra um cego sabel até que vamos. A oxulo filho de egoa alto soso peamos ja mentes ja frentes vinagre que ele quebrarão em balde ja ergo a quante nossa ha ilhos tue busca cordas oculos nosso convento e geju com muito fruta ventre tu já tremes já pias. Seuro santa Maria dinhero me lá darão que é ve esa carta dame mucho que furte cantara Furunando. (6:27)

Besides the generic intercalations already mentioned, there also appear in Gil Vicente linguistic mixtures that enhance the conveyance of marked contrasts characteristic of serio-comic genres. In a great many pieces, *mésalliances* are emphasized by counterposing the dialects of the masses to the the *castiço* usage associated with the upper segment of society. Such mixture is never more evident than in the *Auto dos Reis Magos*, where the dialogues among the rustics, the hermit, and the nobleman accentuate their respective social classes.

Bilingualism, introduced into literature during Roman times, is widely employed by Gil Vicente. Eleven of his extant plays are in Castilian and seventeen others in a combination of Castilian and Portuguese. There is no apparent reason for this other than to please members of the court—all queens of Portugal in Master Gil's time were Castilian—and/or to demonstrate his bilingual abilities.

Another variant of linguistic mixture is the occasional macaronic constructions that our playwright effectively uses for purposes of parody. In addition to the conversation between priest and son in the *Clérigo da Beira*, a good illustration is contained in the jocose sermon (an inserted religious genre) preached by the addled friar at the beginning of the *Auto da Mofina Mendes*. Fragments of religious verses in Latin are personified in the friar's deranged imagination and these "persons" are described in Portuguese:

> Antes disto que dissemos,
> virá com musica orphea
> *Domine labia mea*,
> e *Venite adoremus*
> vestido com capa alhea.
> Trará *Te Deum laudamus*
> d'escarlata hũa libré:
> *Jam lucis orto sidere*
> cantará o *benedicamus*,
> pola gran festa que he.
> (1:133)

After the friar concludes his sermon, the plot shifts to another scene where, in allegorical fashion, the Virgin enters accompanied by her Virtues (Prudence, Poverty, Faith, and Humility). The Virgin asks them to narrate the prophecies they have read. Each complies in turn and gives an account of a known prophecy about the birth of the Messiah. In some of the expositions, verses in Latin, the language of the Church, are combined with the vernacular in what may well be an attempt to authenticate the particular prophecy. Take, for example, Humility's description of the would-be Mother of Christ as revealed by Solomon in his Song of Songs:

> Aqui a chama Salomão
> *toto pulchra amica mea*

> *et macula non est in te.*
> E diz mais, que he *porta coeli*
> *et electa ut sol,*
> balsamo mui oloroso.
> *pulchra ut lilium* gracioso,
> das flores mais linda flor,
> dos campos o mais fermoso:
> chama-lhe *plantatio rosa,*
> *nova oliva speciosa,*
> mansa *columba* Noe,
> estrella a mais lumiosa.

                                                                (1:136)

There is in the Menippea a variety of styles and tones.

Bakhtin argues that stylistic and tonal variety in the Menippea is intensified by the presence of inserted genres. The multifariousness and discordance deliberately created by these intercalated genres contrast with the stylistic unity or, more precisely, the limitation to a single style associated with the epic, the tragedy, lofty rhetoric, and lyric poetry per se.

As observed in the preceding characteristic, the combination of genres does indeed create a plurality of tone and style in Vicentine drama. The prose insertion of the Lord's Prayer in the *Auto da Cananeia* disrupts the cadence of the prevailing verse form. Thus, a sudden alteration of tone is effected, i.e., the unexpected shift from verse to prose lends an air of solemnity to the prayer that would have been impossible had the verse form been maintained.

Concerning Gil Vicente's intercalation of popular and religious songs and the variety of tone and style thereby engendered, António J. Saraiva and Óscar Lopes comment as follows:

Se considerarmos, enfim a obra de Gil Vicente sob o aspecto poético, notaremos a sua diversidade de tons, de temas, de atitudes e de géneros. O lirismo cortês inspira alguns passos delicadíssimos do *D. Duardos,* entre outros. A poesia foclórica está presente sob várias formas: os antiquíssimos cantares paralelísticos, de que Gil Vicente recolheu os últimos exemplares; as serranilhas, as loas tradicionais de Natal; as baladas ou rimances, que imitou além de reproduzir fragmentos, aliás predominantemente espanhóis, e então em moda. A poesia religiosa, ou até litúrgica, está representada por hinos, alguns de inspirações inspiradas nos Salmos ou em outros livros bíblicos: o *Génesis,* o *Livro de Job* ou *Cântico dos Cânticos.*[40]

Although the well-known Portuguese critics include a third type of lyricism (the courtly), it has intentionally been excluded as such from this study since, as it may be verified in the early *Cancioneiros*, many popular songs trace their origin to aristocratic poetry. For our purpose, courtly lyrics are to be understood as included in the popular verse category.

Though perfectly true, these observations do not fully explain how insertion of different genres varies the tone and style of a particular piece. The *vilancete* "Si dormis, doncela," sung by Aires Rosado to Isabel in *Quem Tem Farelos?*, is a fine illustration of the significance of this thirteenth-century characteristic of the Menippea: as the squire sings the verses, his servant Apariço interjects remarks mocking the lyrics.

On the one hand, a melodious composition in the courtly style establishes through its romantic content of a serious and elevated tone; on the other hand, the interjected remarks, stylistically vulgar, typify of the debasing language of the *bas-fonds*. This contrast of expression further reinforces the Menippean preference for oxymoronic combinations.

Perhaps the best case of tonal-stylistic plurality is found in the tragicomedy *Triunfo do Inverno*, where to the naturalistic, versified introduction by Winter early on, another introduction, this time by Spring, is later counterposed in a most delicate and lyrical fashion. For comparative purposes, excerpts from both are presented below:

[Winter]

Sepan todos abarrisco
que yo me soy Juan de la greña,
estragador de la leña,
y sembrador del pedrisco;
cozinero de las papas,
assador mayor de patos
alcahuete de los gatos
y partero de las gatas.

(4:266)

[Spring]

Del rosal vengo, mi madre
vengo del rosale.
. . . .
Afuera, afuera, ñublados,
ñeblina y ventisqueros,
reverdeen los oteros,
los valles, priscos y prados:

> sea el frio rebentado,
> salgan los frescos vapores,
> píntese el campo de flores
> alégrese lo sembrado.
>
> (4:312-13)

Worthy of note, along with the marked contrast of tone and style, is the contrast of content between the two speeches. Winter portrays itself as rugged and rustic, concerned only with the menial toils of the drudge. Spring creates the impression of ladylike refinement that, like a poet, it yearns for beautiful surroundings that bring gaiety and tranquility to the soul.

The irregularity and discontinuity associated with Vicente's drama partially reflect its relation to the Menippea. The presence of interpolated genres (mainly lyric poetry), of the high with the low, of Castilian with Portuguese, of the comic with the serious—in short, of many discordant elements—does break with all traditional dramatic unity much as the Menippea broke with the monotone and rigid high style of the tragedy and epic. Just how aware our dramatist was of the Menippea and its break with classical tradition is beyond the scope of this study. Suffice it to state that carnival, the seasonal festivity from which the Menippea derives its eclecticism as well as all other characteristics, enjoyed a vast popularity during Vicente's time.

The Menippea is distinguished by its feuilletonistic quality.

The last characteristic essential to the Menippea is the genre's topicality and publicistic quality. It could be referred to as the "journalistic" genre of antiquity for its constant involvement with moral and philosophical issues of the day. Bakhtin exemplifies this characteristic thus:

> The satires of Lucian, taken as a group, are an entire encyclopedia of his times: they are full of overt and hidden polemics with various philosophical, religious, ideological and scientific schools, and with the tendencies and currents of his time; they are full of the images of contemporary or recently deceased public figures, "masters of thought" in all spheres of societal and ideological life (under their own names or disguised); they are full of allusions to the great and small events of the epoch; they feel out new directions in the development of everyday life; they show newly emerging types in all layers of society, and so on. They are a sort of *Diary of a Writer*, seeking to unravel and evaluate the general spirit and direction of evolving contemporary life. Just such a *Diary of a Writer* (with, however, a sharp preponderance of the carnivalistic-comic element)

are the satires of Varro, taken in their entirety. We find the same characteristic in Petronius, in Apuleius and others. (*Dostoevsky*, 118-19)

All the representatives of the Menippea are more or less characterized by a feuilletonistic quality that combines organically with all other elements of the genre.

Since it is by now established that Vicente's drama is representative of the Menippea, it is not at all astounding that, like Lucian and others before and since, he relied heavily on satire to render an accurate picture of his society. Satire, after all, is based more on the author's observation of society than on his adherence to a given literary mode.[39] Through this form, he was able to point to and censure the corruption, venality, greed, lust, and ostentation of the various elements that comprised the Portugal of his era.

In the Introduction, we examined how Master Gil satirized all social types of sixteenth-century Portugal. In the ensuing pages, we also detailed his inclusion of the era's open and hidden polemics. These are mostly contained in the dialogical syncrises taking place in numerous locations and surroundings, i.e., from crossroads in undetermined whereabouts to the final "threshold" (the crossing spot to the afterlife). Consequently, there is ample testimony throughout this study of the "encyclopedic" nature of Vicentine drama.

Concluding Remarks

In the preceding pages, the fourteen Menippean characteristics furnished by Bakhtin are applied to Vicentine drama. After discovering that these are not only applicable to his work but permeate it, we reach the conclusion that Master Gil was—with appropriate modifications and complications—a continuator of the serio-comic trend; therefore, a precursor to Rabelais. Had Bakhtin conducted a similar study on the Portuguese playwright, he probably would have shared our conclusion, but it is likely that he was either unaware of Vicente's work or deemed him unworthy of scholarly consideration.

Nevertheless, the application of Bakhtin's critical theories to Gil Vicente has helped us understand the genre and plot-compositional traits and sources of his drama. Up until now, these have been virtually ignored by modern-day Vicentine scholars, the majority of whom have limited themselves to biographical/historical approaches in an effort to explain the playlets as products of a particular epoch—the Middle Ages and/or the Renaissance—and the corresponding literary modes. Traditional approaches of this kind fail wretchedly in explaining apparent thematic and formal parallelisms between our poet's opus and other European works (coeval and ancient alike) of which he, Gil Vicente, was unaware.[40]   Most assuredly, such similarities are not, and could not be, identical; the works must reflect their respective eras and cultures, thereby evincing distinct "external" features.   But it is the "internal" features that remain virtually unchanged and are safeguarded by the genre to which the individual work belongs.   Bakhtin explains the guardian role of genre as follows:

> A literary genre, by its very nature, reflects the most stable, "eternal" tendencies in literature's development. Always preserved in a genre are undying elements of the *archaic*. True, these archaic elements are preserved in it only thanks to their constant *renewal*, which is to say, their contemporization. A genre is always the same and yet not the same, always old and new simultaneously. Genre is reborn and renewed at every new stage in the development of literature and in every individual work of the given genre. This constitutes the life of the genre. Therefore even the archaic elements preserved in a genre are not dead but eternally alive; that is, archaic elements are capable of renewing themselves. A genre lives in the present, but always *remembers* its past, its beginning. Genre is a representative of creative memory in the process of literary development. Precisely for this reason genre is capable of guaranteeing the *unity* and *uninterrupted continuity* of this development. (*Dostoevsky*, 106)

We should not deduce that Master Gil elaborated his pieces with a clear-cut notion of the tradition of genre in which he worked.   Like Rabelais and Dostoevsky, he was not a "stylizer" of any genre. Such a tradition, however, was not altogether unknown to him. Medieval ecclesiastical literature, a descendant of the highly carnivalized early Christian literature, was largely made up of carnivalized genres. Nevertheless, even had he been entirely removed from the mainstream of literary activity of his time, he would have still had access to the most important (perhaps his actual) source of inspiration: carnival itself. This celebration was undoubtedly one of the main conduits through which folk humor impacted upon medieval and Renaissance artistic literature.

Granted that the influence of carnival on literature began to decline at the beginning of the seventeenth century, the tradition of carnivalized genres persists even today.   In Bakhtin's judgment, it is at this point in history that "folk-carnival life is on the wane: it loses touch with communal performance, its specific weight in the life of people is sharply reduced, its forms are impoverished, made petty and less complex" (*Dostoevsky*, 120). That is why when António J. Saraiva remarks that:

assistindo, em 1958, à representacão do *Círculo de Giz Caucasiano*, tive a sensação de ver ressucitado em cena, de uma forma surpreendente e brilhante, um género praticado pelo velho escritor português—um género que eu supunha para sempre sepultado na Idade Média. *(Para a História*, 2:316)

One may very well point out to him that it was not Bertolt Brecht's subjective memory, but the objective memory of the genre in which he composed his plays that preserved its fundamental characteristics through the centuries, characteristics that derive from the incursion of the popular element into the realm of literary creation.

Notes

Introduction

1. Marques Braga, ed., *Obras Completas* (Lisbon: Livraria Sá da Costa, 1978), 4: 122. Henceforth, all quotations from Gil Vicente's plays will be from this collection; therefore, the corresponding volume and page number will be placed at the end of each quotation.

2. For perhaps the most detailed study of iconography in early Iberian literature, see John E. Keller and Richard P. Kinkade, *Iconography in Medieval Spanish Literature* (Lexington: University Press of Kentucky, 1984).

3. Luiz da Cunha Gonçalves, "Gil Vicente e os homens do foro" in *Gil Vicente: Vida e Obra*, ed. Academia das Ciências de Lisboa (Lisbon: n.p., 1939), 241.

4. António J. Saraiva and Óscar Lopes, *História da Literatura Portuguesa* (Oporto: Porto Editora, 1976), 209 (Notes).

5. Anselmo Braamcamp Freire, *Vida e Obras de Gil Vicente* (Lisbon: Edição da Revista Ocidente, 1944), 372.

6. Stephen Reckert, "El verdadero texto de la *Copilaçam* vicentina de 1562," *Studia Philologica: Homenaje ofrecido a Dámaso Alonso* (Madrid: Gredos, 1963), 3: 55-68.

7. J. H. Parker, *Gil Vicente* (New York: Twayne Publishers, 1967), 162.

8. Jack E. Tomlins, "Una nota sobre la clasificación de los dramas de Gil Vicente," *Duquesne Hispanic Review* 3 (1964): 118.

9. Caryl Emerson, trans., *Problems of Dostoevsky's Poetics* (Minneapolis: University of Minnesota Press, 1984), 33-34. Henceforth, all concepts, theories, and analyses in this study will be derived either from this work or from Bakhtin's other monumental work, *Rabelais and His World*, trans. Helene Ilswosky (Cambridge: The M.I.T. Press, 1968).

10. Bakhtin, *Rabelais*, vii-ix. Although the author does not reject in any way Ms. Pomorska's supposition, he nevertheless feels it was the party's vigilance over Russian letters that forced many critics like Shklovsky and Bakhtin to direct their Formalist exegeses along diachronical paths. It should be remembered, therefore, that as structuralist as their theories may seem, Tynianov and Jakobson worked in the same repressive atmosphere, and it was this atmosphere that ultimately shaped their critical theories. Whether Bakhtin himself belonged to the formalist school is a point that can be argued. Tzvetan Todorov makes one of the better observations in this regard: "Bakhtin's relation to (Russian) Formalism is not simple; it blends participation and opposition." See *Mikhail Bakhtin: The Dialogical Principle*, trans. Wlad Godzich (Minneapolis: University of Minnesota Press, 1984).

Chapter 1. The Origins of Peninsular Drama

1. We are purposely omitting Greek tragedy, which has no direct bearing on this study.

2. Reis Brasil, *Gil Vicente e a Evolução do Teatro* (Lisbon: Editorial Minerva, 1965), 12.

3. Fernando L. Carreter, *Teatro medieval* (Madrid: Editorial Castalia, 1976), 10.

4. John Gassner and Edward Quinn, eds., *The Reader's Encyclopedia of World Drama* (London: Methuen and Co. Ltd., 1975), 372.

5. N. D. Shergold, *A History of the Spanish Stage from Medieval Times until the End of the Seventeenth Century* (Oxford: Oxford University Press, 1967), 1.

6. Richard B. Donovan, *The Liturgical Drama in Medieval Spain* (Toronto: Pontifical Institute of Medieval Studies, 1958), 11.

7. Benjamin Hunningher, *The Origin of Theater* (New York: Hill and Wang, 1969), 57.

8. William Tydeman, *The Theater in the Middle Ages* (Cambridge: Cambridge University Press, 1978), 41.

9. Translations within the text are the author's unless otherwise indicated. Excerpts from Vicentine playlets, quotations in Portuguese, and intercalated phrases are not translated. Donovan, *Liturgical Drama*, 14.

10. Tydeman, *Theater*, 42.

11. Winifred Studervant, *Misterio de los Reyes Magos: Its Position in the Development of the Medieval Legend of the Three Kings* (Baltimore and Paris: n.p., 1927), as quoted in Donovan, *Liturgical Drama*, 71.

12. Rafael Lapesa, *De la Edad Media a nuestros días* (Madrid: Editorial Gredos, 1967), 37-47.

13. Shergold, *History of the Spanish Theater*, 6.

14. El Rey Sabio... se propuso la empresa más ambiciosa de crear un nuevo cuerpo legal en que se recogieran las nuevas y avanzadas doctrinas que entonces divulgaban por Europa los romanistas de la Escuela de glosadores de Bolonia: un cuerpo legal que fuera no ya norma de la legislación vigente en el reino, sino luz y guía de las nuevas generaciones de juristas a las que incumbía la ardua labor de organizar y estructurar el Estado con un sentido nacional.
Emilio González López, *Historia de la literatura española* (New York: Las Americas, 1962), 52.

15. Si forte iudicaverint expedire quod fiat Representacio Pastorum, qualiter angelus nunciavit eis Christum natum, dicto psalmo, *laudate dominum de celis usque ad laudate dominum in sanctis eius*, interim sint parati ad altare pueri induti ad modum pastorum. Et tunc illi duo cantores qui regunt chorum incipiant hanc antiphonam *pastores dicite*. Respondentibus pueris *Infantem vidimus*, deinde dicatur *laudate dominum in sanctis eius*. Et sic unoquoque versu repetatur antiphona ut supra dictum est usque ad finem psalmi.
Donovan, *Liturgical Drama*, 49.

16. nin deben ser facedores de juegos por escarnio porque los vengan á ver las gentes como los facen, et si otros homes los fecieren non deben los clérigos hi venir porque se facen hi muchas villanias et desposturas, nin deben otrosi estas cosas facer en las eglesias, ante decimos que los deben ende echar deshonradamientre sin pena ninguna á los que lo fecieren; ca la eglesia de Dios fue fecha para orar et non para facer escarnios en ella: ... Pero representaciones hi ha que pueden los clérigos facer, asi como de la nascencia de nuestro señor Iesu Cristo que demuestra como el angel vino á los pastores et díxoles como era nacido, et otrosi de su aparecimiento como le venieron los tres reyes adorar, et de la

resurreccion que demuestra como fue crucificado et resurgió al tercer dia. Tales cosas como estas que mueven á los homes á facer bien et haber devocion en la fe facerlas pueden: et demas porque los homes hayan remembranza que segunt aquello fueron fechas de verdat; mas esto deben facer apuestamente et con gran devocion et en las cibdades grandes do hobiere arzobispos ó obispos, et con su mandado dellos ó de los otros que tovieron sus veces, et non lo deben facer en las aldeas, nin en los lugares viles, nin por ganar dineros con ello.

Alfonso el Sabio, *Las siete partidas*, Pt. 1, Law 34 (Madrid: n.p., 1807), 276-77. The English translation is by Samuel Parsons Scott, *Las siete partidas*, 2 vols. (New York: American Bar Association, 1931), 1.6.34.

17.   Como a causa de cierta costumbre admitida en las iglesias metropolitanas, catedrales y otras de nuestra provincia, y así en las fiestas de la Navidad de Nuestro Señor JesuCristo y de los Santos Esteban, Juan e Inocentes, como en ciertos días festivos y hasta en las solemnidades de las misas nuevas (mientras se celebra el culto divino), se ofrecen en la iglesia juegos escénicos, máscaras, monstruos, espectáculos y otras diversas ficciones, igualmente deshonestas, y haya en ellas desórdenes, y se oigan torpes cantares y pláticas burlescas, hasta el punto de turbar el culto divino y de hacer indevoto al pueblo, prohibimos unánimes todos los presentes esta corruptela, con aprobación del Concilio, y que se repitan tales máscaras, juegos, monstruos, espectáculos, ficciones y desórdenes, así como los cantares torpes y pláticas elícitas...; asimismo decretamos que los clérigos que mezclasen las diversiones o ficciones deshonestas indicadas con los oficios divinos, o que las consintieren indirectamente..., han de ser castigados.... No se entienda por esto que prohibimos también las representaciones religiosas y honestas, que inspiran devoción al pueblo, tanto en los días prefijados como en otros cualesquiera.
Carreter, *Teatro medieval*, 42.

18.   Donovan, *Liturgical Drama*, 37.

19.   Desde el principio de la Misa salen del Sagrario los Clerizones vestidos de Pastores, y van al Altar mayor por el Postigo, y estan arriba en lo plano mientras se dice esta Misa danzando, y bailando: y acabada la Misa toman Capas los dichos dos Socapiscoles Racioneros para hacer el Oficio de las Laudes, que se empiezan luego en el Coro, a las que habrá tañido el Campanero, segun es costumbre, por la señal que le hicieron, quando se dixere el Hymno *Te Deum laudamus*, con la cuerda del Coro: y dicho por el Preste: *Deus in adjutorium*, desde su silla, se empieza primero la primera antiphona, que es: *Quem vidistis Pastores*: y la dicen toda, y luego los Clerizones hechos Pastores ministrandolos su Maestro Claustrero dicen en el Choro mayor debajo de la Lampara de plata a Canto-llano el verso *Infantem vidimus Pannis involutum, et Choros Angelorum laudantes salvatorem*, y tornan en el Choro a decir toda la antiphona: *Quem vidistis?* y los Pastores responden entre los dos Choros debajo de la Lampara de enmedio el verso *Infantem vidimus, ut supra*, y despues dicen en el Choro tercera vez toda antiphona *Quem vidistis?* y responden los Pastores desde la Puerta del Coro del Arzobispo el verso *Infantem*, y luego salen los Socapiscoles con las Capas de brocado, y Cetros, y llegan a los lados del Aguila del Choro del Arzobispo, y alli los Cantores a Canto-llano les hacen las preguntas siguientes, y los Capiscoles asen de las manos a dos de aquellos Pastorcicos, y les preguntan juntamente con los Cantores lo siguiente:

Canto llanistas.	Bien vengades Pastores, que bien vengades. Pastores do anduvistes? decidnos lo que vistes?
Cantores.	Que bien vengades.

Donovan, *Liturgical Drama*, 32-33.

20.   A 1565 canon from Salamanca categorically forbids *tripudia* (a type of dance) during mass and services. Carreter, *Teatro medieval*, 43.

21.   Donovan, *Liturgical Drama*, 38.

22. Hunningher, *Origin of Theater*, 90.

23. Le Psautier n.° 1151 de la Bibliothèque Municipale de Porto nous offre cependant une petite pastorale, qui prend place à Laudes dans la nuit de Noël. S'adressant aux Pasteurs on leur chante l'antienne classique *Pastores, dicite quidnam vidistis et anunciate Christi nativitatem*. Ici, la rubrique indique *respondeant pastores: Infantem vidimus, pannis involutum, et choros angelorum laudantes Salvatorem*. C'est alors seulement qu'on chante le psaume *Laudate*. La matière de ces deux antiennes, condensée en une seule, forme actuellement notre III.° répons des matines de Noël.
Solange Corbin, *Essai sur la musique religieuse portugaise au Moyen Age, 1110-1345* (Paris: Société d'éditions "Les Belles Lettres," 1952), 294.

24. Luiz Francisco Rebello, *O Primitivo Teatro Português* (Lisbon: Biblioteca Breve, 1977), 35.

25. J. P. Wickersham Crawford, *Spanish Drama before Lope de Vega* (Philadelphia: University of Pennsylvania Press, 1937), 3.

26. J. P. Wickersham Crawford, *The Spanish Pastoral Drama* (Philadelphia: University of Pennsylvania Press, 1915), 14.

27. Ramón Menéndez Pidal, *Poesía juglaresca y orígenes de las literaturas románicas* (Madrid: Editorial Gredos, 1957), 22.

28. Rebello, *O Primitivo Teatro*, 25.

29. Luciana S. Picchio, *História do Teatro Português* (Lisbon: Portugália, 1964), 34.

30. Óscar de Pratt, *Gil Vicente: Notas e Comentários*, 2d. ed. (Lisbon: Livraria Clássica, 1970), 16.

31. Henri Bergson, "Laughter" in *Comedy*, ed. Wylie Sypher (New York: Doubleday Anchor, 1956), 151.

32. Hunningher, *Origin of Theater*, 74.

33. Shergold, *History of the Spanish Stage*, 128.

34. Pratt, *Gil Vicente*, 24-25.

35. Luiz Francisco Rebello, *História do Teatro Português* (Lisboa: Europa-América, 1968), 19.

36. Shergold, *History of the Spanish Theater*, 126-27.

37. Rebello, *O Primitivo Teatro*, 36-37.

38. John E. Keller, "Drama, Ritual, and Incipient Opera in Alfonso's *Cantigas*" in *Emperor of Culture: Alfonso X the Learned of Castile and His Thirteenth-Century Renaissance*, ed. Robert I. Burns (Philadelphia: University of Pennsylvania Press, 1990), 73.

2. The Serio-Comic Genres: A Brief Overview

1. Carolina Michaëlis de Vasconcelos, *Notas Vicentinas* (Lisbon: Edição da Revista Ocidente, 1949), 151-53.

2. "effort de récupération des fêtes populaires originelles, où s'exprimaient un culte des forces naturelles et un esprit individualiste et anarchique." Jean Claude Carriere, *Le carnaval et la politique* (Paris: Le Belles Lettres, 1979), 110.

3. Pensar que en esta vida las cosas della han de durar siempre en un estado, es pensar en lo escusado; antes parece que ella anda todo en redondo, digo, a la redonda: la primera sigue al verano, el verano al estío, el estío al otoño, y el otoño al invierno, y el invierno a la primavera, y así toma a andarse el tiempo con esta rueda continua; sola la vida humana corre a su fin ligera más que el tiempo sin esperar renovarse si no es en la otra, que no

tiene términos que la limiten. *El ingenioso hidalgo Don Quijote de la Mancha*, ed. Luis Andrés Murillo (Madrid: Clásicos Castalia, 1978), 2:400. The English translation is by Samuel Putnam, *The Portable Cervantes* (New York: Viking Press, 1969), 653-54.

4. Putnam, *The Portable Cervantes*, 841. In regard to the carnival elements in this episode, see Augustín Redondo's article "Tradición carnavalesca y creación literaria del personaje de Sancho Panza al episodio de la ínsula Barataria en el *Quijote*," *Bulletin Hispanique* 80 (1978): 39-70.

5. Putnam, *The Portable Cervantes*, 658. "Abrid camino señores míos, y dejadme volver a mi antigua libertad; dejadme que vaya a buscar la vida pasada para que me resucite de esta muerte presente." Murillo, *Don Quijote*, 444.

6. Vistiéronle muy rricos paños de grand valía, / como si fuese dotor en la philosofía; / subió en alta catedra, dixo con bavoquía: / 'D'oy máys vengan los griegos con toda su porfía.' / Vino ay un griego, dotor muy esmerado, / escogido de griegos, entre todos loado; / sobió en otra cathedra, todo el pueblo juntado. / començaron sus señas, como era tratado. Arcipreste de Hita, *Libro de buen amor* (Madrid: Espasa-Calpe, S.A., 1978), 18. The English translation is by Saralyn R. Daly, *The Book of True Love* (University Park: The Pennsylvania State University Press, 1978), 39.

7. Suzana Camargo, *Macunaíma: Ruptura e Tradição* (Sao Paulo: Massao Ohno and João Farkas, 1977), 24.

8. Alexis Salomos, *The Living Aristophanes* (Ann Arbor: The University of Michigan Press, 1974), 36.

9. K. O. Muller, *Literature of Ancient Greece* (New York: Kennikat Press, 1971), 2:7.

10. Lionel D. Barnett, *The Greek Drama* (Edinburgh: Edinburgh University Press, n.d.), 46.

11. Salomos, *Living Aristophanes*, 41.

12. Gilbert Norwood, *Greek Comedy* (New York: Hill and Wang, 1963), 97-106.

13. Salomos, *Living Aristophanes* 42.

14. Camargo, *Macunaíma*, 26.

15. Also see Edward Capps, "Comedy" in *Greek Literature*, ed. Department of Classical Philology of Columbia University (New York: Books for Libraries Press, 1969), 131, and Arthur Pickard-Cambridge, *Dithyramb Tragedy and Comedy* (Oxford: Clarendon Press, 1962), 277.

16. C. M. Bowra, *Landmarks in Greek Literature* (London: Weidenfeld and Nicolson, 1966), 192.

17. Lawrence Giangrande, *The Use of Spoudaiogeloion in Greek and Roman Literature* (The Hague and Paris: Mouton, 1972), 15-16.

18. Ibid., 76.

19. Aristophanes, *Comedies*, ed. The Athenian Society (New York: Rarity Press, 1931), 1:181.

20. Armando Plebe remarks that: "Aristofane sa benissimo che, perché il suo comico sia vivo ed attuale, esso deve nutrirsi della politica e delle sue contese, che son al centro della vita del suo pubblico." See *La nascita del comico* (Bari: Editori Laterza, 1956), 214.

21. Lois Spatz, *Aristophanes* (Boston: Twayne Publishers, 1978), 119.

22. Aristophanes, *Comedies*, 1:193.

23. Charles Paul Segal, "The Character of Dionysus and the Unity of the Frogs"

in *Twentieth Century Interpretations of the Frogs*, ed. David J. Littlefield (Englewoods Cliffs, N.J.: Prentice-Hall, 1968), 55.

24. Aristophanes, *Comedies*, 1:187.

25. Spatz, *Aristophanes*, 120.

26. Aristophanes, *Comedies*, 1:182.

27. Segal, "The Character of Dionysus" in *Twentieth Century Interpretations*, 48.

28. Aristophanes, *Comedies*, 1:210.

29. Ibid., 1:187-88.

30. Ibid., 1:208.

31. Robert Flaceliere, *A Literary History of Greece* (Chicago: Aldine Publishing Co., 1964), 238.

32. Aristophanes, *Comedies*, 1:227.

33. Ibid., 1:252.

34. Aristophanes, *Comedies*, 1:200.

35. Michael Coffey, *Roman Satire* (London: Methuen and Co., Ltd., 1976), 163.

36. Giangrande, *Spoudaiogeloion*, 69.

37. Coffey, *Roman Satire*, 163.

38. Allan P. Ball, *Seneca's Apocolocyntosis* (New York and London: Garland Publishing, Inc., 1978), 60-61.

39. Ibid., 61.

40. For a deeper insight consult Coffey, *Roman Satire*, 165-77.

41. Claudius ut vidit valentem, oblitus nugarum intellexit neminem Romae sibi parem fuisse, illic non habere se idem gratiae: gallum in suo sterquilino plurimum posse. itaque quantum intellegi potuit, haec visus est dicere: "ego te fortissime deorum Hercule, speravi mihi adfuturum apud alios, et si qui a me notorem petisset, te fui nominatarus, qui me optime nosti. nam si memoria repetis, ego eram qui tibi ante templum tuum ius dicebam totis diebus mense Iulio et Augusto. tu scis, quantum illic miserarium contulerim, cum causidicos aduirem diem et noctem, in quos si incidisses, valde fortis licet tibi videaris, maluisses cloacas Augeae purgare: multo plus ego stercoris exhausi. sed quoniam volo." Ball, *Seneca*, 121-22. The English translation is by Ball, 141-42.

42. Ibid., 186-87.

Chapter 3. The Basic Characteristics of the Menippean Satire and Their Application to Vicentine Comedy

1. Sebastião Pestana, *Estudos Gil-Vicentinos* (Sá da Bandeira: Imprex, 1975), 2:99.

2. Gil Vicente, *Tragicomédia de Amadis de Gaula*, ed. T. P. Waldron (Manchester: The University Press, 1959), 35.

3. Aubrey F. G. Bell, *Four Plays of Gil Vicente* (Cambridge: University Press, 1920), xxxvi.

4. Vasconcelos, *Notas*, 385.

5. See *Auto das Fadas*, 5:187.

6. Pestana, *Estudos*, 1:21-22.

7. Vasconcelos, *Notas*, 449.

8. Thomas R. Hart, *Gil Vicente, Farces and Festival Plays* (Eugene: University of Oregon Press, 1972), 19.

9. Gil Vicente, *O Velho da Horta; Auto da Barca do Inferno; A Farsa de Inês*

Pereira, ed. Segismundo Spina (Sao Paulo: Editora Brasiliense, 1965), xxxii.

10. See Bibliography for respective studies.

11. Saraiva and Lopes, *História*, 213.

12. Ibid., 219.

13. Suzanne Dolores Valle-Killeen, *The Satyric Perspective: A Structural Analysis of Late Medieval, Early Renaissance Satyric Treatises* (New York: Senda Nueva de Ediciones, 1980), 185.

14. Pratt, *Gil Vicente*, 247.

15. See footnote in *Triunfo do Inverno*, 4:318.

16. Hart, *Gil Vicente*, 48.

17. Parker, *Gil Vicente*, 68.

18. El espejo que Gil Vicente presenta del hombre tiene dos caras. El poeta, en su carta, se fija principalmente en la naturaleza de este mundo... una vasta composición de oposiciones: lo bueno y perfecto y lo malo e imperfecto. Lo imperfecto "es" (la naturaleza imperfecta del hombre después del Pecado Original) siempre señala a lo perfecto "debe ser" (el hombre como era originalmente al ser creado por Dios). Esta es la idea del hombre en la farsa popular, el hombre en su diaria existencia. Mientras que en el drama religioso Gil Vicente pudo conseguir una clase de humor menor en la ignorancia y simplicidad del pastor ante el pesebre de Belén, evocó la alegría ruidosa de los cortesanos en las farsas, donde la imperfección del hombre es siempre obvia ante la naturaleza del hombre como debiera ser si fuese perfecto, este "debiera ser" siempre a flor de piel. Es la inevitable temática, aunque no necesariamente dramática, expresión de la interacción de contrarios en estas piezas la que da unidad a los dramas religiosos y burlescos de Gil Vicente y suministra una explicación afín del resto de los dramas que por tanto tiempo han sido consternación de los eruditos. Jack E. Tomlins, "Una nota sobre la clasificación de los dramas de Gil Vicente (conclusión)," *Duquesne Hispanic Review* 4 (1965): 13-14.

19. Gil Vicente, *Auto de Moralidade da Embarcação do Inferno*, ed. Paulo Quintela (Coimbra: Atlantida, 1946), xxxii.

20. "¡Moira! ¡no pido mucho tiempo! ¡déjame siquiera este solo día, para indicar a mi mujer alguna cosilla acerca de los dineros y en dónde dejé enterrado el gran tesoro!" Luciano de Samostata, *Novelas cortas y cuentos dialogados*, trans. Rafael R. Torres (Mexico City: Editorial Jus, 1966), 1:306.

21. Bell, *Four Plays*, 120.

22. Eugenio Asensio, "Las fuentes de las Barcas de Gil Vicente," *Estudios portugueses* (Paris: Fundação Calouste Gulbenkian, 1974), 59-77.

23. See Camargo's *Macunaíma: Ruptura e Tradição*.

24. In connection with this seemingly *lapsus calami* and all the controversy surrounding the argument whether the *Auto das Barcas* or *Trilogia das Barcas* was one single play divided into three scenes or three related plays, see the Introduction to Gil Vicente, *Auto da Embarcação da Glória*, ed. Paulo Quintela (Coimbra: Coimbra Editora, 1941).

25. Pestana, *Estudos*, 2:82.

26. Quando si parla della libertà espressiva del teatro gilvicentino, occorre individuarne anzitutto i limiti. Gil Vicente è capocomico e poeta di corte, e al servizio della corte esplica la sua attività: nelle simpatie e nelle antipatie, nella raffinatezza e nella grossonalita del suo specialissimo publico egli trova dunque gli invalicabili confini a quella libertà espressiva che pertanto resta, come per tutti in poeti cortigiani, una libertà condizionata. Gil Vicente, *Comédia de Rubena*, ed. Giuseppe Tavani (Rome: Endizioni dell'Ateneo, 1965), 20-21.

27. Saraiva and Lopes, *História*, 218.

28. Pratt, *Gil Vicente*, 163.

29. Hart, *Gil Vicente*, 44.

30. Maria Zaluar Nunes, "O maravilhoso popular em Gil Vicente" in *Comemoração Vicentina*, ed. University of Lisbon (Lisbon: Imprensa Nacional de Lisboa, 1937), 179. Ms. Zaluar Nunes's article is indispensable for its painstaking documentation.

31. Ibid., 187.

32. Spina, *Gil Vicente*, xxxv.

33. Pratt, *Gil Vicente*, 161.

34. Camargo, *Macunaíma*, 52.

35. Saraiva and Lopes, *História*, 216.

36. F. E. de Tejada Spinola, *As Idéias Políticas de Gil Vicente*, trans. M. de Bettencourt e Galvão (Lisbon: Pro Domo, 1945), 85-86.

37. Hart, *Gil Vicente*, 55.

38. Saraiva and Lopes, *História*, 221.

39. J. Almeida Pavão, *Gil Vicente, Poeta* (Ponta Delgada: n. p., 1963), 75.

40. Carolina Michaëlis de Vasconcelos has done much to dispel the notion that our dramatist was a man of profound learning, well acquainted with the classics with which his own creations share many similarities. See "Nota IV" in *Notas*, 149-507.

Select Bibliography

Alfonso el Sabio. *Las siete partidas*. Madrid: n.p., 1807.

Almeida Lucas, João de. *Líricas de Gil Vicente*. Lisbon: Livraria Clássica Editora, 1943.

Álvarez Espino, Romualdo. *Ensayo histórico-crítico del teatro español desde su origen hasta nuestros días*. Cadiz: La Mercantil, 1876.

Arcipreste de Hita. *Libro de buen amor*. Madrid: Espasa-Calpe, S.A., 1978.

————. *The Book of True Love*. Translated by Saralyn R. Daly. University Park: The Pennsylvania State University Press, 1978.

Aristophanes. *Comedies*. Edited by The Athenian Society. 2 vols. New York: Rarity Press, 1931.

Asensio, Eugenio. *Estudios portugueses*. Paris: Fundação Calouste Gulbenkian, 1974.

Auerbach, Erich. *Mimesis*. Garden City, N.Y.: Doubleday and Co., Inc., 1957.

Bakhtin, Mikhail. *Problems of Dostoevsky's Poetics*. Translated by Caryl Emerson. Minneapolis: University of Minnesota Press, 1984.

————. *Rabelais and His World*. Translated by Helene Ilswosky. Cambridge: M.I.T. Press, 1968.

Ball, Allan P. *Seneca's Apocolocyntosis*. New York and London: Garland Publishing, Inc., 1978.

Barnett, Lionel D. *The Greek Drama*. Edinburgh: Edinburgh University Press, n.d.

Beau, Albin Éduard. *Estudos*. Coimbra: Coimbra Editora, 1959.

Bell, Aubrey F. G. *Estudos Vicentinos*. Translated by António A. Dória. Lisbon: Imprensa Nacional, 1940.

————. *Four Plays of Gil Vicente*. Cambridge: Cambridge University Press, 1920.

Bergson, Henri. "Laughter." In *Comedy*, edited by Wylie Sypher. New York: Doubleday Anchor, 1956.

Bowra, C. M. *Landmarks in Greek Literature*. London: Weidenfeld and Nicolson, 1966.

Braamcamp Freire, Anselmo. *Vida e Obras de Gil Vicente*. Lisbon: Edição da Revista *Ocidente*, 1944.

Braga, Teófilo. "Gil Vicente e as Origens do Teatro Nacional." In *História da Literatura Portugueza*. Vol. 3. Oporto: Chardron, 1898.

Bragança, António. *Lições de Literatura Portuguesa*. 3 vols. Oporto: Livraria Escolar Infante, n.d.

Brasil, Reis. *Gil Vicente e a Evolução do Teatro*. Lisbon: Editorial Minerva, 1965.

————. *Gil Vicente e o Teatro Moderno*. Lisbon: Editorial Minerva, 1965.

————. *Auto da Alma de Gil Vicente*. Lisbon: Escolar, 1965.

Brotherton, John. *The "Pastor-Bobo" in the Spanish Theatre Before the Time of Lope de Vega*. London: Tamesis Books Ltd., 1975.

Burns, Elizabeth and Tom Burns, eds. *Sociology of Literature and Drama: Selected Readings*. Baltimore: Penguin Books, 1973.

Camargo, Suzana. *Macunaíma: Ruptura e Tradição*. Sao Paulo: Massa Ohno e João Farkas, 1977.

Capps, Edward. "Comedy." In *Greek Literature*. Edited by Department of Classical Philology of Columbia University. New York: Books for Libraries Press, 1969.

Carreter, D. Lázaro. *Teatro medieval*. Madrid: Editorial Castalia, 1976.

Carrière, Jean Claude. *Le carnaval et la politique*. Paris: Le Belles Lettres, 1979.

Carvalho, A. L. de. *Gil Vicente: Guimarães Sua Terra Natal*. Barcelos: Vitória, 1959.

Cervantes, Miguel de. *El ingenioso hidalgo Don Quijote de la Mancha*. Edited by Luis A. Murillo. Vol. 2. Madrid: Editorial Castalia, 1978.

Chambers, E. K. *The Mediaeval Stage*. 2 vols. Oxford: Clarendon Press, 1903.

Clark, Katerina and Michael Holquist. *Mikhail Bakhtin*. Cambridge: Harvard University Press, 1984.

Coffey, Michael. *Roman Satire*. London: Methuen and Co., Ltd., 1976.

Corbin, Solange. *Essai sur la musique religieuse portugaise au Moyen Age, 1110-1345*. Paris: Société d'éditions "Les Belles Lettres," 1952.

Cornford, Francis M. *The Origin of Attic Comedy*. Garden City, N.Y.: Doubleday and Co., Inc., 1961.

Crawford, J. P. Wickersham. *Spanish Drama Before Lope de Vega. A Revised Edition*. Philadelphia: University of Pennsylvania Press, 1915.

———. *The Spanish and Pastoral Drama*. Philadelphia: University of Pennsylvania Press, 1915.

Donovan, Richard B. *The Liturgical Drama in Medieval Spain*. Toronto: Pontifical Institute of Medieval Studies, 1958.

Ehrenberg, Victor. *The People of Aristophanes*. New York: Schocken Books, 1962.

Erlich, Victor. *Russian Formalism: History-Doctrine*. Leiden: Mouton and Co., 1955.

Flaceliere, Robert. *A Literary History of Greece*. Chicago: Aldine Publishing Co., 1964.

Frazer, Sir James G. *The Golden Bough: A Study in Magic and Religion*. New York: The Macmillan Co., 1951.

Frye, Northrop. *Anatomy of Criticism*. Princeton: Princeton University Press, 1957.

Garay, René Pedro. *Gil Vicente and the Development of the "Comedia."* Chapel Hill: North Carolina Studies in the Romance Languages and Literatures, 1988.

Gassner, John and Edward Quinn, eds. *The Readers Encyclopedia of World Drama*. London: Methuen and Co., Ltd., 1975.

Giangrande, Lawrence. *The Use of Spoudaiogeloion in Greek and Roman Literature*. The Hague and Paris: Mouton, 1972.

Gonçalves, Luiz da Cunha et al. *Gil Vicente: Vida e Obra*. Edited by Academia das Ciências de Lisboa. Lisbon: n.p., 1939.

Gonçalves Viana, Mário. *Gil Vicente*. Oporto: Editora Educação Nacional, 1937.

González López, Emilio. *Historia de la literatura española*. Vol. 1. New York: Las Americas Publishing Co., 1962.

Gybbon-Monypenny, G. B., ed. *"Libro de buen amor" Studies*. London: Tamesis Books, 1970.

Hamilton-Faria, Hope. *The Farces of Gil Vicente: A Study in the Stylistics of Satire*.

Madrid: Playor, S.A., 1976.

Hardison, Jr., O. B. et al., eds. *Medieval Literary Criticism: Translations and Interpretations*. New York: Frederick Ungar Publishing Co., 1974.

Hart, Thomas R. "Two Vicentine Heroines." *Quaderni Portoghesi* 9-10 (1981): 33-53.

―――. *Casandra and Don Duardos*. London: Grant and Cutler, 1981.

―――. *Gil Vicente, Farces and Festival Plays*. Eugene: University of Oregon, 1972.

―――. "Gil Vicente's Auto da Sibila Casandra." *Hispanic Review* 26 (1958): 35-51.

Herrick, Marvin T. *Comic Theory in the Sixteenth Century*. Urbana: The University of Illinois Press, 1950.

Highet, Gilbert. *The Anatomy of Satire*. Princeton: Princeton University Press, 1962.

Hirschkop, Ken and David Shepherd, eds. *Bakhtin and Cultural Theory*. Manchester and New York: Manchester University Press, 1989.

Hunningher, Benjamin. *The Origin of Theater*. New York: Hill and Wang, 1969.

Keates, Laurence. *The Court Theatre of Gil Vicente*. Lisbon: n.p., 1962.

Keller, John E. "Drama, Ritual, and Incipient Opera in Alfonso's Cantigas." In *Emperor of Culture: Alfonso X the Learned of Castile and His Thirteenth-Century Renaissance*, edited by Robert I. Burns, 72-89. Philadelphia: University of Pennsylvania Press, 1990.

――― and Richard P. Kinkade. *Iconography in Medieval Spanish Literature*. Lexington: University Press of Kentucky, 1984.

―――. *Motif-Index of Medieval Spanish Exempla*. Knoxville: University of Tennessee Press, 1949.

Láfer, Celso. *O Judeu em Gil Vicente*. Sao Paulo: Conselho Estadual de Cultura, 1962.

Lapesa, Rafael. *De la Edad Media a nuestros días*. Madrid: Gredos, S.A., 1967.

Lemos, Maximiano. *O "Auto dos Físicos" de Gil Vicente*. Oporto: Enciclopédia Portuguesa, 1921.

Lida de Malkiel, María Rosa. "Para la génesis del Auto de la sibila Casandra." In *Estudios de literatura española y comparada*, 157-72. Buenos Aires: EUDEBA, 1966.

López Morales, Humberto. *Tradición y creación en los orígenes del teatro castellano*. Madrid: Ediciones Alcalá, 1968.

Lord, Albert B. *The Singer of Tales*. New York: Atheneum, 1978.

Lucian of Samostata. *Lucian's Dialogues*. Translated by Howard Williams. London: George Bell and Sons, 1900.

Martins, Mário. *A Sátira na Literatura Medieval Portuguesa (Séculos XIII e XIV)*. Venda Nova-Amadora: Livraria Bertrand, 1977.

Medvedev, P. N., and M. M. Bakhtin. *The Formal Method in Literary Scholarship: A Critical Introduction to Sociological Poetics*. Baltimore and London: The Johns Hopkins University Press, 1978.

Menéndez Pidal, Ramón. *Poesía juglaresca y orígenes de las literaturas románicas*. Madrid: Editorial Gredos, 1957.

Michaëlis de Vasconcelos, Carolina. *Dispersos Originais Portugueses*. Lisbon: Edição da Revista *Ocidente*, 1969.

―――. *Notas Vicentinas*. Lisbon: Edição da Revista *Ocidente*, 1949.

Miller, Neil. *O Elemento Pastoril no Teatro de Gil Vicente*. Oporto: Editorial Inova,

1970.

Miralles, Carlos. *La novela en la antigüedad clásica.* Barcelona: Editorial Labor, S.A., 1968.

Morson, Gary Saul and Caryl Emerson, eds. *Rethinking Bakhtin: Extensions and Challenges.* Evanston: Northwestern University Press, 1989.

———, ed. *Bakhtin: Essays and Dialogues on His Work.* Chicago and London: The University of Chicago Press, 1986.

Muller, K. O. *Literature of Ancient Greece.* Vol. 2. New York: Kennikat Press, 1971.

Norwood, Gilbert. *Greek Comedy.* New York: Hill and Wang, 1963.

Parker, Jack H. *Gil Vicente.* New York: Twayne Publishers, 1967.

Pavão, J. Almeida. *Gil Vicente, Poeta.* Ponta Delgada: n.p., 1963.

Pellicer, Casiano. *Tratado histórico sobre el origen y progreso de la comedia y histrionismo en España.* Barcelona: Editorial Labor S.A., 1975.

Perry, Ben Edwin. *The Ancient Romances.* Berkeley: University of California Press, 1967.

Pestana, Sebastião. *Estudos Gil-Vicentinos.* 2 vols. Sá da Bandeira: Imprex, 1975.

Picchio, Luciana S. *História do Teatro Português.* Translated by Manuel de Lucena. Lisbon: Portugalia, 1964.

Pickard-Cambridge, Arthur. *Dithyramb Tragedy and Comedy.* Oxford: Clarendon Press, 1962.

Plebe, Armando. *La nascita del comico.* Bari: Editori Laterza, 1956.

Pratt, Óscar de. *Gil Vicente: Notas e Comentários.* Lisbon: Livraria Clássica, 1970.

Putnam, Samuel. *The Portable Cervantes.* New York: The Viking Press, 1969.

Ramalho, Américo da Costa. *Estudos sobre a Época do Renascimento.* Coimbra: Instituto de Alta Cultura, 1969.

Rebello, Luiz Francisco. *O Primitivo Teatro Português.* Lisbon: Biblioteca Breve, 1977.

———. *História do Teatro Português.* Lisbon: Publicações Europa- América, 1968.

Reckert, Stephen. *Gil Vicente: espíritu y letra.* Madrid: Editorial Gredos, 1977.

———. "El verdadero texto de la Copilaçam vicentina de 1562." In *Studia Philologica: Homenaje ofrecido a Dámaso Alonso,* Vol. 3., 53-68. Madrid: Gredos, 1963.

Redondo, Agustín. "Tradición carnavalesca y creación literaria del personaje de Sancho Panza al episodio de la ínsula Barataria en el Quijote." *Bulletin Hispanique* 80 (1978): 39-70.

Remédios, Mendes dos. *Conferências sôbre os Autos de Gil Vicente.* Coimbra: Coimbra Editora, 1923.

Révah, I. S. "L'Auto de la Sibylle Cassandre de Gil Vicente." *Hispanic Review* 27 (1959): 167-93.

———. *Recherches sur les oeuvres de Gil Vicente.* 2 vols. Lisbon: Ottosgrafica, Ltd., 1951.

Rocha Brito, A. da. *A Farsa dos Físicos de Gil Vicente.* Coimbra: Coimbra Editora, 1937.

Rose, H. J. *A Handbook of Greek Literature.* London: Methuen and Co., Ltd., 1948.

Ruiz Ramón, Francisco. *Historia del teatro español desde sus orígenes hasta mil novecientos.* Madrid: Editorial Alianza, 1967.

Salomos, Alexis. *The Living Aristophanes*. Translated by Alexis Salomos and Marvin Felheim. Ann Arbor: The University of Michigan Press, 1974.

Sandbach, F. H. *The Comic Theatre of Greece and Rome*. London: Chatto & Windus, 1977.

Saraiva, António José and Óscar Lopes. *História da Literatura Portuguesa*. Oporto: Porto Editora, 1976.

Saraiva, António José. *Para a História da Cultura em Portugal*. Vol. 2. Lisbon: Europa-América, 1961.

―――. *Gil Vicente e o Fim do Teatro Medieval*. Lisbon: Editorial Inova, 1944.

Saraiva, José Hermano. *Ditos Portugueses Dignos de Memória*. Lisbon: Europa-América, 1979.

Scott, Samuel P. *Las siete partidas*. 2 vols. New York: American Bar Association, 1931.

Shergold, N. D. *A History of the Spanish Stage from Medieval Times until the End of the Seventeenth Century*. Oxford: Oxford University Press, 1967.

Sinclair, T. A. *A History of Classical Greek Literature*. New York: Haskell House, 1973.

Spatz, Lois. *Aristophanes*. Boston: Twayne Publishers, 1978.

Spitzer, Leo. "The Artistic Unity of Gil Vicente's Auto da Sibila Cassandra." *Hispanic Review* 27 (1959): 56-77.

Stacy, R. H. *Russian Literary Criticism: A Short History*. Syracuse: Syracuse University Press, 1974.

Stathatos, Constantine C. *A Gil Vicente Bibliography (1940-1975)*. London: Grant and Cutler, 1980.

Sticca, Sandro. *The Latin Passion Play: Its Origin and Development*. Albany: State University of New York Press, 1970.

Tejada Spinola, F. E. *As Idéias Políticas de Gil Vicente*. Translated by M. de Bettencourt e Galvão. Lisbon: Pro Domo, 1945.

Teles, Maria J. et al. *O Discurso Carnavalesco em Gil Vicente*. Lisbon: GEC Publicações GEC, 1984.

Teyssier, Paul. *Gil Vicente: O Autor e a Obra*. Lisbon: Biblioteca Breve, 1985.

―――. *La langue de Gil Vicente*. Paris: Librairie C. Klincksieck, 1959. Thompson, Stith. *Motif-Index of Folk Literature*. Bloomington: Indiana University Press, 1955.

Todorov, Tzvetan. *Mikhail Bakhtin: The Dialogical Principle*. Translated by Wlad Godzich. Minneapolis: The University of Minnesota Press, 1984.

Tomlins, Jack E. "Una nota sobre la clasificación de los dramas de Gil Vicente." *Duquesne Hispanic Review* 3 (1964): 115-31, and 4 (1965): 1-16.

Tooke, William. *The Dialogues of Lucian*. London: The Navarre Society, n.d.

Tydeman, William. *The Theater in the Middle Ages*. Cambridge: Cambridge University Press, 1978.

University of Lisbon. *Comemoração Vicentina*. Lisbon: Imprensa Nacional, 1937.

Valle-Killeen, Suzanne Dolores. *The Satyric Perspective: A Structural Analysis of Late Medieval, Early Renaissance Satiric Treatises*. New York: Senda Nueva de Ediciones, 1980.

Van Rooy, C. A. *Studies in Classic Satire and Related Literary Theory*. Leiden: B. J. Brill, 1965.

Vicente, Gil. *Copilaçam de Todalas Obras*. Edited by Maria L. Carvalhão Buescu.

2 vols. Lisbon: Imprensa Nacional, 1983.

———. *Obras Completas*. Edited by Marques Braga. 6 vols. Lisbon: Sá da Costa, 1976.

———. *Comédia de Rubena*. Edited by Giuseppe Tavani. Rome: Edizioni dell'Ateneo, 1965.

———. *O Velho da Horta; Auto da Barca do Inferno; a Farsa de Inês Pereira*. Edited by Segismundo Spina. Sao Paulo: Editora Brasiliense, 1965.

———. *Comedia del Viudo*. Edited by Alonso Zamora Vicente. Lisbon: Publicações do Centro de Estudos Filológicos, 1962.

———. *Tragicomédia de Amadis de Gaula*. Edited by T. P. Waldron. Manchester: Manchester University Press, 1959.

———. *Auto da Barca do Inferno*. Edited by Charles D. Ley. Madrid: Instituto Antonio de Nebrija, 1946.

———. *Auto da Embarcação do Inferno*. Edited by Paulo Quintela. Coimbra: Atlântida, 1946.

———. *Copilaçam de Todalas Obras de Gil Vicente* (Lisbon, 1562), reprinted in facsimile as Obras completas de Gil Vicente. Lisbon: Biblioteca Nacional, 1928.

———. *Farsa de Inês Pereira*. Edited by F. J. Martins Sequeira. Lisbon: Livraria Popular de Francisco Franco, n.d.

Index